GRAND PRIX
Yesterday & Today

This edition published in 2010
10 9 8 7 6 5 4 3 2 1

Text and design © Carlton Books Limited 2010

A CIP catalogue record for this book is available from the British Library.

ISBN 13: 978-1-84732-592-1

Editor: Nigel Matheson
Designer: Ben Ruocco
Production: Lisa French
Picture Research: Tom Wright

Printed in Singapore

GRAND PRIX
Yesterday & Today

BRUCE JONES

CARLTON
BOOKS

Contents

Foreword by Sir Stirling Moss

It has been my pleasure and honour to have been in involved in Formula One racing for more than 50 years, first as a competitor then as a spectator and I can't think of a sport that has changed as much as motor racing yet remained exactly the same. It is still a matter of the fastest around the track and first past the chequered flag, but that is pretty much where the similarities end. In my day, we didn't have computers to tell us if the brake fluid was overheating by a couple of degrees or fourth gear was sticking, we drove the car on feel and instinct.

This is where *Grand Prix: Yesterday and Today* is so special. On every spread there are two pictures, one from days gone by and the other modern, each depicting a similar theme. It gives you the chance to see how things have changed for the driver, the pit crew and the spectator.

The changes in safety are, of course, fantastic. It was commonplace for the grid to be missing a driver every year because he had tragically perished in a racing accident; now it has been more than a dozen years since Formula One has mourned a fatality on the track. But then there is the other side, the formal presentations of today are so different to the almost ad hoc awards of a trophy to the race-winner in my day. It was a more innocent age.

However you look at it, the technology may have changed but the spirit of needing to be the fastest still remains. And that is the joy of motor racing.

Ciao

Clearly the darling of the fans, Emerson Fittipaldi really looks the part with his sunglasses and sideburns as he waves the national flag and they shout their support ahead of the 1973 Brazilian GP at his home circuit, Interlagos. The equipment and environment have changed out of all recognition, but the passion to win remains as strong today as it was in the first grand prix at Le Mans in 1906

Introduction

TIME MOVES ON AND NOTHING IS ever the same. Yet, a century after Grand Prix racing began, there remains one central tenet that has changed not one jot, that battle of man and machine to be first to the finish.

It's always a pleasurable activity to delve through old photos, but in compiling *Grand Prix Yesterday & Today* it was an exceptional delight to find not just forgotten images or never-before-published shots of racing from early in the 20th century, but to realise how much hadn't changed. Yes, put Emerson Fittipaldi and Kimi Raikkonen side-by-side and there's little similarity between a dark-skinned Brazilian with notable sideburns and insect-eye sunglasses with a fair-skinned, boy-like Finn from three decades later. But their desire to win is no different, and this trend runs through every facet of the sport.

This is key, as although it's easy to laugh at the behemoths with which Grand Prix racing began at Le Mans in 1906, or the cotton racing suits and flat caps sported by the stars of the 1930s, it should always be remembered that Grand Prix machinery has always been cutting-edge, the best of its time. Yes, a 1950 Alfa Romeo looks huge next to a tiny, sharknose Ferrari from 1961 and a wedge-shaped JPS Lotus positively crude when compared to a 2005 McLaren, but this only goes to emphasise how the Grand Prix scene never stands still. One peep inside a contemporary cockpit demonstrates that admirably, with enough gadgetry on the steering wheel alone seemingly to launch a rocket, whereas the early racers were fortunate to have even one gauge, and they had to reach outside the cockpit to change gear, rather than simply flicking a paddle on the steering wheel.

Equipment aside, what has changed more than anything else is attitude and, with it, accessibility. Put simply, Grand Prix paddocks of yesteryear were open to all, the drivers always ready to sign a proffered autograph book. And even more ready to don their suits and party the night away, untroubled by the intrusion of the press. In fact, it was expected of them. Take British World Champions Mike Hawthorn in the 1950s and James Hunt two decades later: they were celebrated for their party lifestyle, most feeling that it added to the glamour of the sport. In short, the public wanted to see Grand Prix racing stars as gladiators. When it comes to those who attracted limitless admiration for the way that they stared death in the face, Tazio Nuvolari and Gilles Villeneuve stand out.

This brings me on to the subject of safety, one that has been dealt with so successfully that drivers can now walk away from accidents twice as large as ones that would have killed them but two decades ago. Indeed, death has been all but banished since Ayrton Senna's death shocked the sport in 1994, whereas it lurked around almost every corner through the sport's early years. Even looking through grid shots from the 1960s and 1970s makes you realise just what a terrible roll call racing claimed. Look at the cars now, the clothing too and especially the circuits, and it's clear to see why the odds were against survival in the early years, with cobbled surfaces and tracks lined either with trees or precipitous drops. You can't help but feel that the tracks of old - even the tracks of today as they were a few decades ago - had more character, but it's understandable why they had to change, with spectators moved back from the action so that giant gravel-traps could be inserted.

It's said that money makes the world go round, and in few sports can this be as true as it is in Grand Prix racing, with the costs of being competitive being sky-high compared to the early days. Certainly, it has never been a cheap game, but the costs are stratospheric now. However, the rewards are greater too. After all, you can't imagine Michael Schumacher having to charge around on a scooter in his late 70s to check out his property portfolio as his equivalent from 40 years earlier, Sir Stirling Moss, does.

Finally, praise must go to the LAT photo agency in Teddington, source of each and every one of the photos used in this book, as it's an absolute gem and the hardest part of the photo research was to limit myself to one photo from the 50 or more that I could have picked for each selection.

Bruce Jones

One
Kings of Speed

Right: Drivers came in all shapes and sizes in 1962. Here, Salvadori, Surtees, de Beaufort, Maggs, Ireland, Clark and Hill listen in at a drivers' briefing at Monza

1950

The speed merchants

THE QUICK AND THE VERY QUICK is perhaps the most applicable phrase to describe grand prix racing drivers. Those that fit into the very quick category are not those merely crowned world champion but those who are multiple world champions. They have proved beyond doubt that their sheer ability at the wheel was the main factor in their success, rather than simply being lucky to have been driving the best car.

Step forward Juan Manuel Fangio, who swept to five world titles in the 1950s, and Jim Clark, who bagged a brace in the 1960s before he died at the wheel. Jackie Stewart carried the standard into the 1970s, before Alain Prost and Ayrton Senna stood out in the 1980s and early 1990s. But then along came Michael Schumacher who blew away almost every record in the book. By the end of 2004, the German ace had seven world titles to his name. His rivals had to settle for merely being quick.

Right: It's safe to say that Juan Manuel Fangio looks more middle-aged than young go-getter after winning the 1950 Monaco GP, but boy could he drive...

Far right: It took the athletic genius of Michael Schumacher and the might of Ferrari to overhaul the Argentinian's record number of world titles in 2003

1953

F1's nearly men

THE ULTIMATE BADGE IS WORLD CHAMPION, yet some of the very greatest drivers won races by the handful yet somehow never landed the crown. Stirling Moss stands out in these ranks and, close on half a century later, being described as "the greatest driver never to have been world champion" must still rankle more than a little. Yet that's precisely what he is. The speed and the race craft was there in buckets, but unluckily for Moss so was Juan Manuel Fangio, collecting his five world crowns when at least a couple ought to have gone the Englishman's way.

Ronnie Peterson looked to be a successor to Moss's title. But even the great Swede's reputation is overshadowed by a driver who hit Formula One with an instant impact just before Peterson was killed at Monza in 1978. This was Canadian wild child Gilles Villeneuve, a driver who redefined bravado. There was nothing he couldn't do with a car, except win a world title... although perhaps the fact Ferrari provided him with cars that handled like trucks rather than racers had something to do with it.

Left: It's early days as Stirling Moss still has a full head of hair, but his particular poise and focus is already clear at the French GP in 1953

Right: Gilles Villeneuve is all boyish looks, but he could make a racing car handle like no-one else. Sadly, death overtook him at Zolder in 1982

1951

Old hands and young guns

THE CULT OF YOUTH is plain to see in all sports in the twenty-first century and the fact that the fathers of some of today's grand prix racers are younger than the race winners of old is startling proof of this. Take the two most extreme cases. On the one hand, Louis Chiron raced on in Formula One until he was 54, before deciding to take things easy. However, he couldn't stay away and the Monegasque holds the record for being the oldest driver to contest a grand prix at fully 55 years, nine months and 19 days in 1955. Still he wanted more and failed in his final attempt to qualify for his home grand prix in 1958, just short of his 59th birthday.

Compare this to Fernando Alonso who made his Formula One debut at 19, before becoming the youngest-ever grand prix winner at 22 years and 26 days and then outstripping Emerson Fittipaldi's record from 1972 of being the youngest World Champion by more than a year, aged just 24 years, one month and 27 days. Perhaps starting in karting at four had something to do with this.

Right: Lewis Hamilton made an instant impact when he hit Formula 1 at the age of 22, winning three grand prix before the year was out

Far left: Louis Chiron puts his 52 years' experience to good use in arguing a point with his mechanic in 1951

1953

Fit to drive

ATHLETES WHO SIT DOWN is one way to describe today's grand prix racers, but it only provides half the picture since the likes of Michael Schumacher, David Coulthard, Mark Webber and Jarno Trulli in particular are hyper-fit, trained exhaustively so that they can maintain focus through the course of a grand prix, minimizing mistakes. However, this hasn't always been the case.

Back in the 1950s, drivers came in all shapes and sizes with the likes of the 'Pampas Bull', Jose Froilan Gonzalez, far from svelte. However, do not for one instant consider the drivers of yesteryear less impressive sportsmen because the cars they drove were physically more tiring, the races longer and they were more exposed to the elements. The difference is that today's drivers have to endure greater G-forces in acceleration, braking and cornering, which is why they train and train when not racing or testing.

Left: Mark Webber (middle) cuts an athletic dash at a Williams launch at the start of the 2005 season with Antonio Pizzonia (left) and Nick Heidfeld

Far left: Who ate all the pies? Well, judging by Jose Froilan Gonzalez's girth in 1953, it could well have been him, but it didn't stop him from winning

1958

Getting on

FRIENDSHIP AND SPORT ARE NOT MUTUAL in the upper echelons of any sport. Blame the curse of money as sport represents big business. Indeed, many a professional sportsperson feels that their worth is ranked as much by the money that a team is prepared to pay them as by results achieved. As equipment is inevitably not equal, the true guide to a driver's form is to compare their pace to that of their team-mate, which is why so few team-mates are buddies...

There are always a few exceptions. David Coulthard, Jenson Button and Jacques Villeneuve are three kindred spirits who not only knock about together while living in Monaco between the races, but even eschew hotels when at the events and line up their luxury motorhomes together in the paddock. The earlier days were more carefree, however, with parties at every grand prix and no partnership was closer than that of English drivers Mike Hawthorn and Peter Collins. They were inseparable. But, such was the way of the sport, that both died before they reached 30.

Left: Mike Hawthorn and Peter Collins were great friends and partied wherever they went, giving grand prix racing a yet more glamorous image

Right: Jacques Villeneuve and Jenson Button (pictured), along with David Coulthard, are friends not only at home in Monaco but at the circuits as well

1964

Facing the press

CAN'T LIVE WITH 'EM, CAN'T LIVE WITHOUT 'EM is how many people involved in Formula 1 feel about the press as they fret about their constant intrusion, exasperated by their insatiable appetite for insight and comment on everything. Yet the teams' sponsors are fully aware that publicity is their lifeblood. It's the reason they dig deep into company coffers to display their names on the cars. Plus, ultimately the fans want to know everything from the technical pointers to the gossip.

The biggest change of all is in the sheer number of media people who attend every race. It's no longer just a handful, but a cast of several hundred and the competition between this army of journalists and photographers ups the ante. Not only do they want the information, but they want it immediately as the internet waits for no-one. Some drivers cope with this ceaseless barrage with charm and humour, others less so.

Left: Jim Clark eyes up a journalist's less-than-portable tape recorder when cornered for an interview in the early 1960s

Right: Fernando Alonso found himself subjected to the full glare of media interest through 2007 as he warred with his team and team-mate

1962

Bossing it

NURTURE VERSUS NATURE is a debate related to the bringing up of children, but it has its place in the grand prix world as well in the relationship between the team boss and his driver. Some are famously tough, such as the relationship John Surtees had with the Ferrari management in the 1960s, when nurture clearly didn't enter into their vocabulary. Not that this single-minded, former motorcycle champion is a figure who needed TLC, but while Enzo Ferrari was still alive, it was something of a Ferrari trait to treat the driver merely as an employee.

The flip side of the coin is the team chiefs who bring the best out in their star drivers by nurturing them. Think Lotus chief Colin Chapman with Jim Clark in the 1960s, Ken Tyrrell with Jackie Stewart in the 1970s and McLaren's Ron Dennis with Mika Hakkinen in the 1990s. Most obvious of all is the flamboyant Flavio Briatore who coaxed Michael Schumacher to his peak in the mid-1990s and then guided Fernando Alonso to glory in 2005. Briatore offers his stars bear hugs like none before him.

Right: Few partnerships have ever been as close and successful as the one formed between Lotus boss Colin Chapman and his protege Jim Clark

Far right: It's safe to say Renault's Flavio Briatore and Fernando Alonso had a close relationship, until Alonso signed for McLaren for 2007...

1960

Racing wives

DRIVERS AREN'T MARRIED in the imagination of most grand prix racing fans. Instead, drivers lead a dashing life on the road "chasing crumpet" as Stirling Moss memorably describes what he got up to during the 1950s. Contemporary Mike Hawthorn was another ladies' man and their partying was typical of the age.

Yet times change and the drivers' choice of female company is now limited by the automatic gates at the paddock entrance that refuse entry to anyone without an officially sanctioned pass. Smiling prettily at the gatekeeper is no longer an option. Perhaps this is why most of today's crop of drivers are married, many with children. One thing is for sure, however: today's racing wives are no longer expected to take an active role by helping time their loved one's progress by operating a brace of stopwatches. Instead, Corinna Schumacher and Connie Montoya simply offer company to Michael and Juan Pablo when the drivers aren't on the track, in technical debriefs or pressing the flesh at sponsorship functions but can do little else. Time is short and their role reduced, but at least the increased safety of the cars means that racers' wives and girlfriends can expect their loved ones back in their arms at the end of the day.

Left: Betty Brabham glances at her stopwatch and, judging by her expression, husband Jack has just missed out on pole position at Oporto in 1960

Right: Being hauled into a celebratory team photo-shoot is about as close as Michael Schumacher's wife Corinna gets to the heart of the action

26

1967

All in the family

THE FAMILY COMES ALONG FOR THE RIDE wasn't always the modus operandi for the top stars of grand prix racing. Indeed, with drivers being killed so frequently until the 1970s, this was probably a good idea. However, some drivers wouldn't contemplate going racing without their entire family accompanying them. One of the most visible such drivers was Graham Hill who not only had wife Bette on the stopwatches, but Brigitte, Damon and Samantha in tow. This sort of upbringing was always going to make the children either love the sport or hate it, and it clearly inspired Damon as he went on to become the first son of a World Champion to repeat his father's feat in 1996.

It appeared that fellow English driver Nigel Mansell was happier for his sons Greg and Leo to have taken their sporting ambitions into golf, Nigel's favoured retirement pastime, rather than racing. But, lo and behold, Greg and Leo announced at the start of 2006 that they too would like to race cars. Think how hard it is for a racing driver father to say no in such circumstances.

Left: Graham Hill with future champion Damon in the foreground, Brigitte on the right and Samantha being looked after by a nanny in the background

Right: After a childhood spent watching his father Keke compete, Nico found that their roles were reversed when he himself hit F1

1968

Fathers and sons

KEEP IT IN THE FAMILY. This is the only way to explain why so many sons of racing fathers also take up motor racing. Of course, having spent their childhood going racing every second weekend and ducking in and out of the pits and the paddock, to many it's seen as a natural way of life. However, with the death of so many racers in the first half of the twentieth century, one can't imagine it being their mothers' first choice of profession for their offspring.

Alberto Ascari – World Champion in 1952 and 1953 – followed in the wheel tracks of his father Antonio and was spookily killed in almost identical circumstances. Fortunately, it has been a happier story for other sons of racing drivers such as 1980 World Champion Alan Jones outperforming his father Stan. His own son Christian is also a racer, as are the progeny of former World Champions Emerson Fittipaldi, Niki Lauda, Jody Scheckter, Keke Rosberg and Nelson Piquet. Recently the most successful sons of all have proved to be World Champions Damon Hill (1996) and Jacques Villeneuve (1997).

Left: Jackie Stewart offers a few teasing hints about being a grand prix driver to his elder son Paul in 1968

Right: Thirty-two years later and Jackie and Paul are partners, running their own Formula One team, Stewart Grand Prix, before selling it to Ford

Above: If Ricardo and Pedro Rodriguez look implausibly young as they hit the international scene, it is because they were. Here they are at the Sebring in 1961 before either made it to the grand prix scene

Right: The most successful pair of brothers ever, Michael and Ralf Schumacher, celebrate their one-two at the 2001 French GP, but Ralf appears destined to live for ever in Michael's shadow

1961

Brothers

SPORTING SIBLINGS are often led by the eldest one who is fired by a genuine desire to pursue a dream. Sadly, the second in line are seldom as successful, although there are a few exceptions. Younger Jody Scheckter outshone older brother Ian for example.

The Rodriguez brothers from Mexico took the racing world by storm in the late 1950s when they starred on the international sports car racing scene at the age of 17 and 15. Ricardo, the younger, was the first to enter Formula One – with Ferrari no less – and he qualified on the front row on his debut. A year later he was dead. Pedro took longer to blossom, but the sport killed him, too.

The Fittipaldis, Wilson and Emerson, possess a similar story, but both are fortunately still with us, with Wilson's son Christian also making it onto the grand prix scene.

Which brings us to the Schumacher brothers. Nothing comes close to their grand prix record in terms of success and notoriety, with Michael currently the sport's only seven-time World Champion and Ralf a six-time race-winner to date.

1992

The trappings of success

MONEY MAKES THE WORLD GO ROUND. Nowhere is this truer than in the world of Formula One. The hybrid cars cost a fortune to build and a further fortune to run. In the early days this cost was borne by the motor manufacturers, who recouped it off the back of their road car sales. From the 1950s on, however, the manufacturers have tended to be outnumbered by the specialist teams. But one factor that has risen out of all proportion is how much the drivers are paid. Take Michael Schumacher, motor racing legend, who pockets more than £1 million per grand prix.

Racing drivers have always loved toys. First comes the fast car or two or three, then the swanky house, perhaps a private jet and, almost inevitably, a yacht, most likely moored in the harbour at Monaco, just in view of their apartment. They live in a parallel world. However, not all use their money on frippery. David Coulthard and Eddie Irvine have made sound business investments, although both are amateurs compared to Jody Scheckter who sold an arms training company he'd started in the USA for $60 million.

Right: Long retired from racing, John Surtees proudly displays the spoils of winning world championship titles on both two wheels and four

Far right: The trappings of success are more easily earned now. This is David Coulthard in front of the Columbus Hotel in Monaco which he co-owns

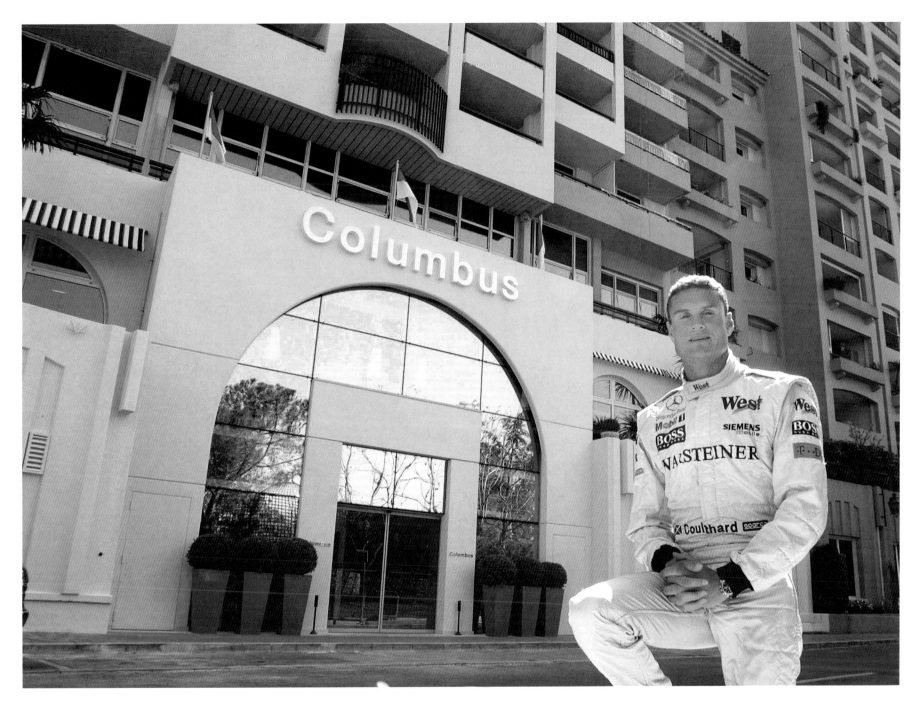

The victory wave

IT'S THE MOMENT OF TRUTH, the moment that every television director looks for and the moment when a driver signals to the world at large that the job is done and the race is won. In the early days of racing, it was a mere raise of the hand to acknowledge the chequered flag. Over the years, however, it is becoming ever more dramatic. In fact, some of today's racers would probably try to stand in celebration were they not so firmly anchored into their seat by their safety harness. Take Michael Schumacher's routine, now seen on more than 80 occasions, when the punching of the air with both hands is followed by an alternate pumping action. Dignified it ain't, but you can't mistake the emotion.

Famously, there was one occasion when the raised arm salute was performed to convince the race officials that a particular driver was the winner. This was at the Italian GP in 1971 when Peter Gethin emerged through a five-car pack to pip Ronnie Peterson. It was so close that Gethin used this bit of kidology to encourage the judges to pick him as the winner. It worked and he won by 0.01s. And it's a good thing it did as he never won again.

Left: BRM's Peter Gethin punches the air to convince the officials that he has just won the 1971 Italian GP in the closest finish ever. It was to be his only victory

Right: Lewis Hamilton is ecstatic as he crosses the finish line in Montreal in 2007 for the first of his grand prix wins

1960

On the podium

IT'S NOW CENTRAL TO THE SHOW, but the grand prix podium used to be something of an afterthought. Many circuits didn't have a tailor-made podium until the last 30 years or so, something that would have today's television directors pulling their hair out in horror. The photographers wouldn't be too happy either.

In grand prix racing's earlier days, the podia were little more than low platforms with the crowds kept back by a polite rope cordon. The drivers were decked with a huge garland, handed their trophies – often of truly magnificent scale in the pre-war days – and would wave to the assembled crowd before heading off humbly to get changed into their dinner jackets and go off to the post-race formal dinner. Back then, there was none of today's choreographed champagne spraying, no leaping in the air and not a single television interview or debrief to keep them behind.

Left: Jenson Button had experienced the top step of the podium only once before 2009, but during his title-winning season he became a regular

Far left: The backdrop to the podium is certainly more than a little rudimentary at the 1960 United States GP, but Stirling Moss doesn't appear to mind

1978

All together now

MOTOR RACING IS A TEAM SPORT. Sure, the driver takes the plaudits, but the effort is not solely seen in the cockpit. Success is a long process. First there is the inspiration entering the designer's head, followed by the engineers working out this new car's best method of construction and then the development of the car through testing with the endless toil of the army of mechanics.

The victory celebrations of the winning team, like the podium celebrations, are becoming ever more effusive. Blame it on Lotus principal Colin Chapman, who started a habit in the early 1970s of leaping over the pit wall – they weren't topped with fences then – and flinging his cap in the air if one of his cars won. Nowadays, celebrations appear to be the preserve of the mechanics as they rush across the pitlane and scale the safety fence to get a vantage point from which to wave to their hero. Upstaged, the team chiefs stay at ground level for the first of a series of interviews.

Right: Lotus chief Colin Chapman turns to celebrate with his crew after Ronnie Peterson has headed home a Lotus one-two at Zandvoort in 1978

Far right: Smiles all round as Fernando Alonso and the Renault crew signal the fourth win of his 2005 campaign after he triumphed in the European GP

1966

Champagne moments

POP GOES THE BUBBLY. It seems as if drivers have always let rip with a shower of Champagne after winning Grand Prixs but it hasn't always been thus. It would always be consumed, often in some quantity, but it was never sprayed until the late 1960s. The change occurred after Dan Gurney won the Le Mans 24 Hours in 1967 and decided to spray some. Champagne lovers may have originally quaked at this sacrilege, but the ejaculation of the fizzy stuff is now synonymous with sporting celebration. Perversely, the spraying of Champagne is banned in France.

The unleashing of a Champagne shower is something of an art form and also a crafty way for a driver to get one over his boss at a time of negotiation by pouring a wave of fizz down his back. Alternatively, others use it as a chance to get one back on a driver who has beaten them and a sharp blast of bubbles into their face leaves them blinded momentarily and their eyes stinging. For the likes of Renault's Flavio Briatore, a man who puts about the image that he bathes in the stuff, it's simply party time.

Left: Champagne consumption on the podium was dignified in the 1960s. This is Jack Brabham after winning the 1966 French GP

Right: Ayrton Senna was a driver of intense emotion and the podium ceremony was often the first time he relaxed all meeting. Gerhard Berger gets a faceful of bubbly

1970

The spoils of victory

IT'S NOT TRUE THAT ALL THAT REMAINS of a win is the entry in the record books. Victory has always been rewarded with prize money. In fact, the teams covered the majority of their costs with a combination of this and starting money until the 1970s. Now, the importance of victory is translated into points that are accrued towards a championship challenge. This, in turn, has a distinct mercantile value of its own since a team's ranking dictates precisely how much of the official travel fund is allocated to their coffers for the following season.

The one constant is the trophy, with the biggest reserved for the winner. Those awarded in the early days of the sport were huge, highly individual pieces of silverware or occasionally ceramic, but, sadly, today's trophies are altogether less grand. Indeed, a rule was passed in the 1980s that trophies be small and light enough so that the more elderly dignitaries presenting them wouldn't struggle. Bless!

Left: Jochen Rindt uses all of his strength to lift a simply marvellous piece of silverware after winning the 1970 British GP at Brands Hatch for Lotus

Right: The trophies these days are more standard and less distinctive. This is Kimi Raikkonen's steering wheel-shaped one at the 2005 Hungarian GP

1985

The autograph men

SIGN HERE, SQUIRE. This is essentially the cry from grand prix racing fans since the show began in 1906, although you can be sure that the requests were probably a little more reverential in those early years. The autograph is a treasured item, especially if the driver who has taken your pen is really a hero. When access to the paddock was free and easy up until the 1960s, landing an autograph was simply a matter of waiting politely. Since then, however, it has been a matter of subterfuge or waiting pressed against a fence surrounding the hallowed paddock.

With the accessibility of the drivers plummeting since grand prix paddocks were gated, the desire for autographs is soaring. No longer is it good enough to gain the hard-to-decipher response in an autograph book. These days, fans come to races armed with framed photographs, race programmes, team clothing or, occasionally, a proffered breast or midriff. The majority have a value, as all save the breast or midriff can be sold to the highest bidder on eBay.

Left: Johnny Herbert ignores the fact that it's a Ferrari cap and signs for an enterprising fan during his walk from the paddock at Monaco in 1996

Far left: Williams ace Nigel Mansell adds considerable value to a fan's crash helmet at the scene of his first grand prix win, Brands Hatch, in 1985

1962

Meeting the public

DRIVERS HATE THEM, but PR duties are part of the reason they are paid so highly in the twenty-first century. Jacques Villeneuve famously bucked this trend by having a clause written into his contract with BAR that he would do only four days of PR duties per year. This was in stark contrast to his good friend David Coulthard, who appeared to do that many in a fortnight, being flown around the globe to press the flesh wherever McLaren's sponsors did business. Combine this with their testing duties and it's small wonder that some drivers feel more than a little overstretched.

However, it wasn't always the case and, until the 1970s, drivers weren't expected to do much at all, except perhaps attend a post-race cocktail party, which they'd have done anyway. Look at photos of the early PR exercises and there's a wonderful innocence about them. Good grief, some of the drivers look as though they are actually enjoying what they've been asked to do.

Right: Why party when you can race cars? Jim Clark, Jo Bonnier, Graham Hill and Ricardo Rodriguez play Scalextric one evening at the Dutch GP

Far right: McLaren's Mika Hakkinen and David Coulthard get stuck into a PR event for engine supplier Mercedes at the German GP in 1999

47

1970

Back in the saddle

SOME DRIVERS ARE NEVER THE SAME after a big crash. The total belief in their ability and the strength of the car around them is knocked. It's fractional but it might make the difference between being a race winner and an also-ran. A classic case is Johnny Herbert who appeared the best around on his approach to Formula One, but his physical and mental injuries following a horrific, near foot-severing accident at Brands Hatch left him short of fulfilling his potential.

One of the most remarkable features of racing drivers, however, is their ability to buck all suggested recovery timescales from horrendous injuries to get back on the track. Niki Lauda is the most outstanding example of this. Conferred the last rites in hospital after suffering horrendous burns in the 1976 German GP, he was back racing again just six weeks later in his determination to defend his lead in the World Championship. That he finished fourth that day was testament to his will power.

Left: Graham Hill is still wheelchair-bound after breaking his legs in the 1970 US GP, but finds it amusing to join a nurses' picket line

Right: Niki Lauda came back from near-death in 1976 to race again, heavily burned, after missing just two grands prix. He prepares for the Fuji finale

1970

Last respects

THEY WERE ONCE A REGULAR FEATURE of a grand prix driver's diary, but mercifully the perpetual improvement in car strength and circuit safety meant that, by the 1980s, funerals had become the exception to the rule. No longer is the dark suit and black tie kept ready in case they're needed to celebrate the life of a fallen friend or contemporary. Sadly, drivers from the early years of grand prix racing until the 1960s could expect to use theirs all too often.

The most remarkable funeral of all was Ayrton Senna's after he was killed at Imola in 1994. The superstar sportsman's sudden death rocked his home country, Brazil, to its roots and a national day of mourning was declared. Funerals and memorial services can be both woefully sad and yet beautiful at the same time, which perhaps explains why Nelson Piquet once commented at one: "I hope that mine is as beautiful as this." Fortunately, that day has yet to come.

Left: All is sombre as Nina Rindt follows the pall-bearers carrying her husband Jochen's coffin after he was killed in practice for the 1970 Italian GP

Right: A minute's silence in memory of Roland Ratzenberger on the grid at Imola in 1994. Cruelly, Ayrton Senna was to crash fatally within the hour

Two
Magnificent Machines

Right: One of the bravest of the brave, Camille Jenatzy has a huge smile on his face at the 1906 French GP as his Mercedes 120 roars into action

1951

Side view

COMPARE AND CONTRAST grand prix cars over the past century and you'll realize they've changed out of all recognition, from head-up two-seaters with driver and riding mechanic to low-down, computer-honed thoroughbreds. Every grand prix racer since 1906 may be light years away from its contemporaries driven on the road, but regular design advances over the last 100 years have made grand prix cars from 1906 look like dinosaurs next to today's road rockets.

Seen from the side, it's clear how designers continually strive to make the most of every breath of air that passes over the car from nose to tail. Compare the bluff front of the 1951 vintage Ferrari 375 with the F2001 from the same stable 50 years later. Aurelio Lampredi, designer of the 375, interrupted its smooth flanks only to add venting to keep the front-mounted engine cool. The F2001, on the other hand, is all wings, winglets and bargeboards to push the airflow over the top of the car, around the wheels and then on to the rear wing for the much-desired downforce.

Left: Alberto Ascari's bluff-fronted Ferrari 375 was the pace-setter in the 1951 Spanish GP at Pedralbes, starting from pole position. Notice how high the driver sits in the open-sided cockpit, with no roll-over protection

Below: Michael Schumacher is all but hidden in his Ferrari F2001, but look at how the wings, bargeboards in front of the sidepods and winglets ahead of the rear wheels push the airflow here, there and everywhere

1954

Head-on

SLEEK BUT PURPOSEFUL is the best description of a grand prix designer's desire for the frontal design of their racers. One of the keys to making a car go faster is the minimization of its frontal area and designers have made them smaller and smaller in that respect. Refining the car to a point is an obvious route to take, but then the wheels would be left sitting up in the airflow. This is why Mercedes took the route of enclosing them in 1954 before the practice was outlawed to keep grand prix cars distinct from sportscar racers.

Racing car designers never stop trying to produce the most aerodynamically efficient car on the grid. Look at the cars of today and you'll see how the wheels are still great, obtrusive, solid lumps, but how the designers shape sundry wings to channel the airflow. In McLaren's case, they've even added vestigial wings to the side of the airbox, offering as much downforce as possible while keeping the passage of air to the rear wing as clean as possible.

Right: Formula One cars like never before or since. In the 1954 Spanish GP, these Mercedes W196s sport wheel-enclosing bodywork, since outlawed

Far right: With rules rewritten so that all four wheels must be exposed, here in 2005 they're shown clearly out in the airflow around the McLaren MP4-20

1962

Rear ends

FROM CLEAN TO CLUTTERED is a good way of describing the transformation of the hindquarters of grand prix cars since their early days. Blame it on the aerodynamicists. The elegant boat tails that existed from the early days through until the 1960s now seem elegance personified. When cars were front-engined, they boasted a delicate tapering end and a smooth rump. When the engines were moved to the tail in the late 1950s, they sported a point through which you'd see the gearbox and the exit of the exhaust pipes.

This all changed when aerofoil wings were added in 1968; these were growing in height and extravagance before being kept in check. The transformation of the tail didn't end there as designers were led by Lotus's Colin Chapman to consider the passage of air under the car as well as over it. The result was the rear bodywork continuing out beneath the rear wing and later the arrival of black under-car trays, known as diffusers, that kicked up at the tail in a messy assortment of channels, removing all semblance of elegance.

Left: Formula One cars of the early 1960s were tiny and sleek, as shown by Roy Salvadori's neat Lola as it sits on the grid before the 1962 Dutch GP

Right: Almost obscured by its massive rear wing, Nigel Mansell's class-of-the-field Williams makes sparks fly in second place at the 1992 Monaco GP

1969

Taking off

ON A WING AND A PRAYER was the case in the late 1960s when grand prix designers discovered that fixing a wing or two to their cars transformed the handling. Working on the principle that they wanted the opposite of the upward force an aeroplane designer wants, they simply fixed the same-shaped wing upside down. The force generated would push the car down onto the track – something that is crucial for handling.

Brabham tried this first in 1968 with initial rear wings soon augmented by wings at the front, both fixed directly to the cars' suspension. The trouble was that, as these wings were mounted on ever-higher supports, they became fragile and broke as downforce generated exceeded their engineering. Soon outlawed, the designers reshaped their thinking and since then have come up with an increasing number of wacky ideas, albeit many are outlawed in order to keep cars' speeds in check.

Above: The Arrows A22 of 2001 surprises onlookers at Monaco with this peculiar extra wing mounted above the nose of the car. It was never seen again

Left: Crazily high-mounted wings front and rear are the order of the day for Brabham at the 1969 Spanish GP with Jack Brabham leading Jacky Ickx

1958

Driving force

MORE HORSEPOWER PLEASE has been the cry of racing drivers ever since that first grand prix at Le Mans in 1906. Back then, the way of achieving as much power as possible was to run engines of gargantuan cubic capacity with lumps of more than 20 litres not unusual among the field. These were necessary as the cars were built for strength rather than lightness. Gradually, as lightness became more important, smaller engines were utilized, although the nadir of grand prix racing came after 1960 when their capacity was reduced to a measly 1500cc.

The most remarkable thing about engine design is that every time the sport's governing body changes the rule book to reduce maximum engine size in order to slow the cars, the engine builders find another way to extract more horsepower. Chief among these is making the engines rev faster and the V8s introduced for 2006 expected to rev at close to 20,000rpm. As for peak power, they're never likely to match the 130bbhp, three-lap qualifying specials fitted at the peak of the turbo wars in the 1980s.

Right: Engines looked so simple and basic back in the 1950s. This is the V6 in the nose of Ferrari's 1958 Dino 246. Note the natty box of spark plugs

Far right: By 2007, engines were less attractive to look at, but were masterpieces of packaging, being light and compact for a low centre-of-gravity

1966
Letting it all out

EVERY STYLE IMAGINABLE has been utilized over the years in an effort to make effective exhaust pipes for grand prix racers. Up until the engines were moved from the nose to the tail in the late 1950s, however, the exhaust was typically just one enormous pipe fixed to the side of the car. It ran beneath the scalloped entry to the cockpit and was wide enough to blow a tennis ball through.

Then they became altogether less obvious as they simply stuck out of the back of the fared engine cover. The best period for exhaust fetishists was after 1966 when a host of teams fitted V12 engines with banks of pipes running to the tail. Ferrari and Honda were chief among those who appeared to model theirs on tangled spaghetti. Huge rear wings and ever more rearward bodywork then covered their form and, by the late 1990s, exhausts had all but disappeared as they were plumbed out of the top of the sidepods, with the glorious pipes of old replaced by a simple air vent.

Left: By 2005, as aerodynamicists started tucking exhaust pipes away, all you would see was their point of egress through the tail of the top bodywork

Far left: This V12-engined Honda RA273 illustrates how exhaust pipes were a work of art in 1966. We really dig those striped overalls too, guys

1976

Getting a grip

THE ROLE OF TYRES in grand prix racing is crucial. Those who don't appreciate their worth deride them as simply something to keep the wheels off the ground, but recent racing shows how the extra speed delivered through tyre development is the most effective way of shaving chunks off a car's lap time.

Early racers used solid tyres. They had the advantage of not succumbing to punctures, but offered precious little grip and a rock-hard ride. The advent of pneumatic tyres was a huge step forward, but the quantum leap came in the early 1970s when, increasingly, wide tyres were replaced with slicks – racing tyres without so much as a groove cut in their smooth surface. Slick tyres achieved extraordinary grip levels, although the teams still fitted tyres with a tread if it was wet. This is how they remained until 1998 and a decision to slow cars introduced a simple fore-and-aft groove in the standard dry weather tyre, cutting effectiveness by reducing grip.

Left: Grooved rubber had become the order of the day by the start of the twenty-first century. This is Michelin's dry weather tyre in 2005

Far left: Slicks or treadless tyres were all the rage in the 1970s. This is James Hunt's title-winning McLaren M23 in the 1976 Belgian Grand Prix

1951

The cockpit

LEATHER SEAT, SIMPLE DIALS AND LOW SIDES made up the cockpit of a grand prix racer until the mid-1950s. Without a rollhoop behind the driver's head, there was no need for seatbelts as an inversion meant beheading and drivers preferred to be thrown clear of cars that all too frequently burst into flames. The cockpit was a simple place and an environment into which fans could peer as the drivers came past, noting their different driving styles as they tackled corners. Some were laid back, steering with a twitch of the wrists, while others were more muscular with a flash of arms and elbows.

With car safety advancing and aerodynamics becoming more of a factor, drivers found themselves effectively built into the car with little more than their head protruding above the car's flanks. In fact, the designers wanted the drivers to occupy as little space as possible as they were not deemed design-efficient. Some took this to extremes with taller drivers left so little space in which to operate that they'd get cramp. The drivers were certainly safer, however, with the cockpit being a safety cell in the case of a major accident.

Right: There's space aplenty to waggle your elbows in this 1951 Alfa Romeo 159. Note the scarily placed fuel tank on the right and the solid-state gear lever

Far right: Rubens Barrichello shows how the driver was squeezed into a high-sided cockpit by 2009, with all controls on the steering wheel

1937

The steering wheel

THE BIGGER THE CAR, THE BIGGER THE WHEEL holds true in racing car design. It makes sense since a large wheel offers more leverage to help hurl a big brute around a corner, particularly a big brute that seems allergic to cornering as the early grand prix cars were. These days, however, a steering wheel is much more than simply a device for making a car turn.

Having been downsized all the way through to the 1980s, the steering wheel remained a simple tool, but then the designers decided to put as many controls as possible just in front of the driver. With paddles fitted on the rear of the steering wheel for up and down gear shifts, a driver's hands never had to leave the wheel. Better still, all manner of electronic gadgetry was included, enabling a driver to check on his car's condition without having to peer at the small gauges of old that were perpetually hidden by their flashing hands.

Left: With space increasingly limited in the cockpit, it was decided to put the controls on the wheel itself, including gearchange paddles on its reverse side

Far left: Simple and purposeful is the order of the day with this Auto Union C with Hermann Muller holding a large steering wheel for a large car

1959

Onboard refuelling

A DEHYDRATED DRIVER MAKES MISTAKES. Well aware of this during the longer grands prix in the early days of the sport – the 1906 French GP was made up of two six-hour heats – teams ensured that the drivers were given a drink if they stopped at the pits. Sitting behind giant engines that roasted their feet in the cockpit, drinks were vital to keep drivers awake and 100 per cent focused.

Perhaps one of the simplest and most dramatic advances in driver safety is the fitment of the humble drinks bottle. Using an electric pump, it powers the chosen drink up a tube and through the front of a driver's helmet into his mouth. For the past couple of decades, this liquid has been an isotonic mixture laced with anti-cramping salt concocted by a team dietician. Dieticians are highly valued in driver preparation as all the team's investment could be wasted if a driver is unable to perform at his best.

Above: External catering was the norm until the arrival of drinks bottles in the 1970s. This is Ian Burgess taking on liquid in the 1959 French GP

Right: Narain Karthikeyan, Jordan driver in 2005, shows how liquid is now always on tap through a small tube in the chinbar of the helmet

1935

Race clothing

THE DRIVER'S WARDROBE early in the last century was made up of a stout jumper and perhaps a jacket, but since drivers were lowered into increasingly contained cockpits this has changed. Not surprisingly, fire – the element that claimed as many lives as violent impact – also altered the way that a driver dresses.

The simple cotton overalls that drivers wore after World War One were finally replaced in the 1960s with the advent of flameproof material and textile technology that carried across from the aerospace industry. Its tradename was Nomex and this was soon crafted into three-layer overalls worn atop fireproof underwear, making the driver hot but safe. Indeed, with their faces covered by full-face helmets, there is little way for body heat to escape, but it's better to be safe than sorry. These overalls are also beloved of sponsors as a billboard for their logos.

Left: Lightweight cotton suits are much in evidence at the drivers' briefing at Monaco in 1935, albeit chiefly to keep oil off the drivers' clothes

Right: Contemporary race overalls are made out of multiple fireproof layers and are also an excellent way of showing off the sponsors' logos to the TV viewers

1932

Helmets

CLOTH AND CORK. It's hard to believe, but these were once considered suitable materials out of which to make a driver's headwear. Cork was only introduced in the early 1950s, moulded into shape over a form to make a windproof head covering, occasionally with a visor fixed to its sun peak in place of the goggles that had kept the wind out of the drivers' eyes since racing began.

Then, in the 1960s, safety became an issue, rollhoops were fitted and glassfibre was used in place of dope-soaked cork. The pudding-bowl shape was also superseded, with Dan Gurney one of the first to introduce a full-face helmet in the mid-1960s. The next step was the fitment of a fireproof padded lining and then a built-in air supply activated if the car's fire extinguisher was triggered. Taking driver safety to ever-increasing levels, helmets then had to pass a stringent impact-testing regime before being passed fit for use in grand prix racing. Now, with radio earpieces as standard, a driver can even receive messages from his pit crew.

Right: Like the early race overalls, helmets used to be more for keeping wind and insects at bay than for impact protection. This is man-of-the-moment Tazio Nuvolari's cloth example with his race goggles atop

Far right: The contemporary crash helmet is full-faced, impact-tested and fireproof. It's personalized too, so any fan will be able to identify these as Fernando Alonso's and Giancarlo Fisichella's by their colour schemes alone

1968

Holding tight

GETTING A GOOD GRIP is a must for grand prix drivers. Not just around corners, but also on the steering wheel and the pedals. Drivers, therefore, have always worn gloves, not necessarily the string-backed type worn by sporting motorists until the 1960s, but ones that ensure the rim of the steering wheel sits firmly in their hands. They are also designed to protect the palms of gear-changing hands in the longer races or races in which there were more than the usual number of gearchanges, such as Monaco. Later on, as with all items of apparel, these became fireproof.

In the early days, footwear wasn't a matter of importance, but as the cars became lighter and cornered with more aplomb by the end of the 1950s, drivers relied on lightweight shoes to enable them to get the feel of the pedals through the soles of their feet. These too have long since been replaced by fireproof boots that cover the ankle and offer the thin soles demanded by the drivers.

Left: Jackie Stewart is typical of many drivers in the 1960s, sporting lightweight leather shoes (or boots)

Right: Soon, though, all race boots were manufactured from fireproof material and worn, of course, over fireproof socks for safety

Above: It's a safe to say that the unveiling of a car used to be rather low-key, as shown by this laid-back McLaren reveal for new sponsor Yardley in 1972

Right: When Honda launched its RA107, it was introducing a marketing concept as well as its new car

1972

Unveiling a new car

IT CAN BE THE FLASHIEST ELEMENT OF A MODERN SEASON, but the unveiling of a new car or perhaps a sponsor can be an aurora of lasers, an explosion of sound and a burst of photographers' flash guns. If done right, it's theatre, very expensive theatre. If not, it's an embarrassment. But it hasn't always been so...

Indeed, in the days before sponsors, teams simply used to push their latest charger out of the back of their transporter and get straight on with testing. More is expected these days, as shown by teams taking their new challenger to such dramatic locations as the classical amphitheatre Taormina in Sicily simply to provide the right backdrop. They fly in the press too, as that's the whole point of a launch: to gain maximum exposure for all parties concerned. For teams such as Ferrari, though, a corporate image runs through what they do and their launches are more about continuity than impact. While, left to their own devices, out-and-out racers Williams would rather simply roll the car out of their transporter and get on with the serious business of going fast.

Three

Trackside

Right: One of the greatest sights in racing: the old downhill start at Spa-Francorchamps as Tony Brooks leads away at the start of the 1958 Belgian GP

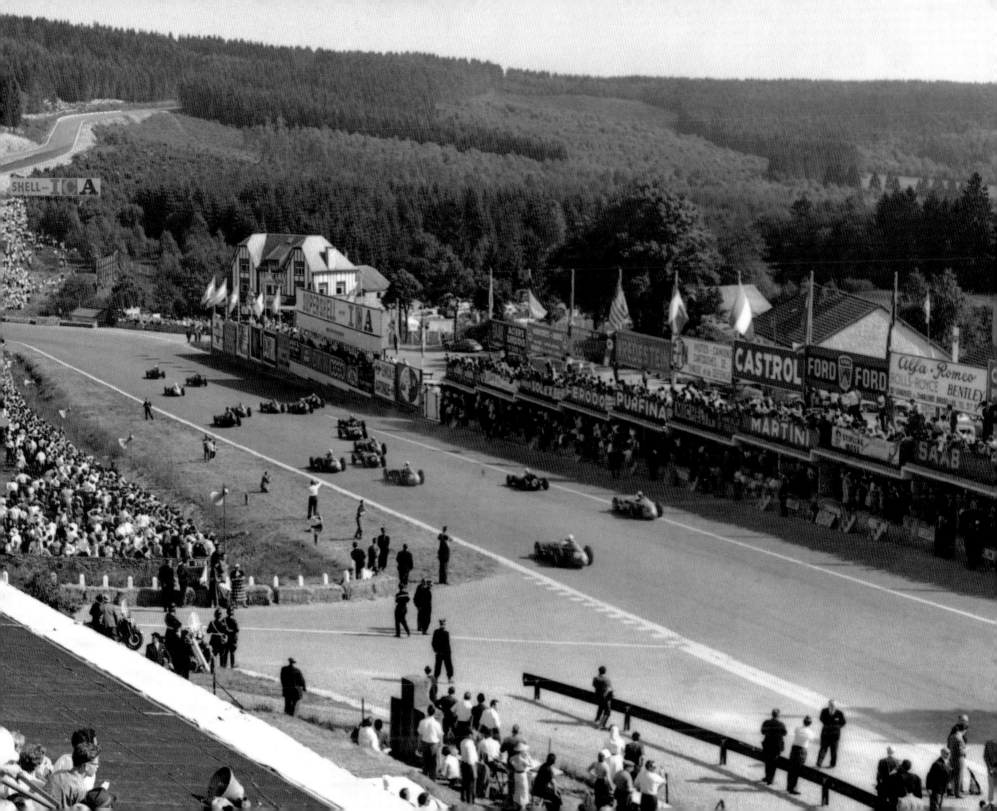

1937

Donington Park

IT DIPS AND IT DIVES, it twists and it turns and it's a massive part of British motorsport heritage. Donington Park is only in existence today because of one man: Tom Wheatcroft, a very wealthy motor racing enthusiast. He was first excited by racing at the very circuit he now owns when the all-conquering Auto Union and Mercedes-Benz came across to England in the late 1930s and crushed our home-grown machinery. These silver German racers were in another league, pushing out so much horsepower that they took off over the crests. But then the war came and the circuit dropped into decline.

Having made his fortune in the building trade, Wheatcroft bought the dilapidated venue to store an ever-expanding collection of old racing cars. One thing led to another and a shortened version of the circuit reopened for racing in the late 1970s. Its crowning glory came with the hosting of the Grand Prix of Europe in 1993 at which Ayrton Senna put on one of the virtuoso performances of the modern age.

Left: It's 1937 and Manfred von Brauchitsch steers his Mercedes W125 through Donington's Old Hairpin in pursuit of Auto Union's winner Bernd Rosemeyer

Right: Ricardo Patrese guides his Benetton past the same point in 1993, on F1's only visit to the circuit since the World Championship began in 1950

1957

The run-off

A MARGIN FOR ERROR didn't always exist in motor racing. Indeed, leave the circuit at speed in the early days of racing and the chances are that what followed would either hurt you or, sadly, kill you. Mistakes were costly. However, that has long since been

considered unacceptable and the introduction of run-off – an area between the track's edge and the barriers beyond – allows racers to make minor mistakes and run wide without ending their race or even their life.

If you compare tracks today with those of yesteryear, spectators are now far further away from the racing surface, often with a grass verge between the track and the crash barriers. It's at the corners, however, that the difference is most stark, with deep beds of gravel in situ to slow cars that have fallen off. Evolution is constant and gravel beds are being superseded by areas of similar expanse in which large swathes of tarmac are used instead of small stones, so that drivers can slow their cars by spinning them, instead of ending up bogged down.

Above: One slip and a driver would be off into the trees at the Nurburgring. But this isn't a driver liable to make mistakes, it's Juan Manuel Fangio rounding the banked Karoussel in 1957, racing to his greatest victory

Right: This shot from the grandstands at Sepang in 2005 shows how much gravel there is to catch the fallen. It's even colour-coded so they can judge just how much they messed up their braking for the corner…

1967

The Nurburgring

SOME CALL IT "GREEN HELL". It's safe to say that the full Nurburgring – the Nordschleife – is the big one. It's more than 14 miles in length and it has 174 corners as it twists through the Eifel Forest. Some of these are blind, others make the cars airborne and two are so steeply banked that they make the drivers' teeth chatter. It's amazing that it took until 1976 for grand prix drivers to consider it too dangerous for Formula One as the cars became faster by the year.

Their argument was proved right in that very race, with world championship leader and main campaigner for its removal from the calendar, Niki Lauda, nearly succumbing to burns suffered when he crashed on the opening lap. Racing still continues on the Nordschleife to this day, but Formula One didn't return until the mid-1980s when a thoroughly modern and considerably shorter circuit was built in the area around the start/finish straight. It's a shadow of its former self, because it was designed with safety in mind.

88

Above: Adjudged too dangerous for Formula One, the Nordschleife was replaced with this modern version over part of its course with no runs through the trees and run-off aplenty

Left: The Nordschleife layout of the Nurburgring – clocking in at more than 14 miles – was in use until 1976. Jackie Stewart crests one of its awesome jumps in his BRM in 1967

1952

Spa-Francorchamps

MANY CALL IT THE GREATEST TRACK OF ALL. The drivers love it. Sure, the weather at Spa-Francorchamps can be capricious, with torrential and incredibly localized rain a likelihood rather than a rarity, but it's a circuit with majesty and with mighty terrain as it sweeps through the Ardennes hills. The corners really make the drivers work for their living. Perhaps the most daunting of all is Eau Rouge, a corner entered at speed from a downhill straight into a left kink at the foot of the hill that feeds directly into a right-hand twist as the track fires up a steep incline. The ride isn't over yet, as the cars go light when the slope eases off just when they need to start turning left again at the crest. Entry speed is important, but exit speed even more so, as it feeds onto the track's longest straight.

Getting Eau Rouge right is great, a real buzz for drivers who dare to take it flat out. Many, however, have got it wrong. In BAR's first season, 1999, both of their cars were destroyed there as Jacques Villeneuve and Ricardo Zonta came to grief on the corner's exit in huge, spectacular accidents.

Right: One of the most famous descents in grand prix racing, the drop from La Source to Eau Rouge and sharply up again. The Ferraris lead away in 1952

Far right: And this is 2005, emphasizing how little has changed, which makes this stretch of track one of the few to have held on to its defining character

1955

Banked corners

IT IS BIG IN AMERICA, but circuits with banked corners have all but dropped from view in Europe. Brooklands in Surrey was the first this side of the Atlantic, but its day was run before World War Two. Avus on the outskirts of Berlin was another, but that too has long since been broken up, although images live on of Tony Brooks's Ferrari running high around its brick-built slopes to victory in the 1959 German GP.

The most famous of all is Monza, the eternal home of the Italian GP. In its heyday, it was a circuit of many track configurations, with a circuit on the infield that included a huge, steeply banked turn at either end of its oval shape. This could run exclusively or be added to the flat outer circuit, as it was for the 1955, 1956, 1960 and 1961 Italian GPs. But then the banking was deemed too dangerous and dropped out of favour, which began its descent to its present sorry state, just a flash of something caught by the television cameras as the cars rush into the first chicane on the outer circuit. Only when Indianapolis opened its doors to the World Championship again in 2000 did a short segment of banking get used by grand prix cars again.

Far left: Banked corners have been all but dropped by grand prix racing on the grounds of safety. This shot shows a pair of Mercedes at Monza in 1955

Left: Years later, that glorious Monza banking lies defunct and unloved alongside the current circuit, serving only as a reminder of what used to be

1921

Grandstands

SHARING YOUR RACE VIEWING with others by sitting in a grandstand is the accepted way for most racegoers to watch a grand prix. Not only do spectators get a superior view of the circuit by sitting up high in the steeply banked grandstand, but they get to share the experience with those sitting around them.

This ought to be a pleasure as they are invariably like-minded people sharing a common interest in racing.

Most circuits place their main grandstand opposite the pitlane, as it's a popular place to be when the cars assemble on the starting grid before taking the start. Equally, if there's a close finish, spectators are in the right place to see who crosses the line first. Other popular grandstands are at the world's great corners, such as Eau Rouge at Spa-Francorchamps, Stowe at Silverstone and Casino Square at Monaco.

The best grandstands of all are the ones that line the stadium section at Hockenheim, where grandstands face grandstands, permitting a wall of noise generated by 100,000 airhorn-blaring fans.

Above: Since racing began, people wanted to make sure that they could see the best of the action. These flag-topped grandstands are at Le Mans in 1921

Right: The competition nowadays is to make the grandstands look as stylish as possible. This shot was taken at the Shanghai International Circuit in 2005

1924

Advertising banners

WIN ON SUNDAY, SELL ON MONDAY is a mantra oft-repeated by the car manufacturers involved in motorsport and adding a sporting image to their products is a sure-fire way of making them more attractive. However, it's not only the manufacturers who want to be seen in and around grands prix. The very first ones ran 'nude', but long before the advent of TV, companies appreciated the power of adding their logo to trackside hoardings. Sure, they weren't as corporately clinical as today's advertising banners, but there were plenty of them.

The style of adverts has changed over the years and today's trackside banners are strictly controlled by a special management company and are very, very expensive. They can afford to be since their net worth is extraordinary due to the gargantuan worldwide TV audience. The rules surrounding these trackside ads are extremely stringent and considerable study is expended in making sure that they are as visible as possible to the TV cameras.

Above: Trackside signage is nothing new. Take a look at this corner on the Le Mans road circuit in 1924, festooned with advertising banners long before the advent of TV

Right: Advertising is now strictly controlled, with only major corporate advertisers invited to pay to place their logo on any of the bridges or gantries that cross each circuit

1967

Crowd protection

A LENGTH OF ROPE OR A HAY BALE is no longer deemed sufficient to keep racing cars from inadvertently escaping and meeting the racing fans. Any photograph of grand prix racing from its inception until the late 1960s shows this could have happened at almost any time. Yes, there were dark moments, such as Wolfgang von Trips crashing into the crowd early in the 1961 Italian GP and meeting his death along with 14 of the spectators. But there could easily have been many, many more, especially as the early cars were so enormous and would have taken some stopping.

Race organizers eventually realized that not only would crash barriers around their circuits keep the cars contained and their drivers safe, but that they would no longer run the risk of those unwanted, potentially sport-threatening headlines, that racing kills spectators. That's to say nothing of the litigation that would follow. So, bit by bit, the crowds have been pushed back further from trackside and contained behind wire-mesh fences. It's certainly less intimate, but it's the only way to go.

Left: Nowadays, there are debris fences everywhere, which is a setback for amateur photographers, but a major step forward for safety

Far left: Knowing no better, the fans at Monaco in 1967 presume these straw bales will keep them safe as Denny Hulme dives inside Mike Spence

CAR	NAME	TIME	TIME	M.
1	J. CLARK	1-?:?	1-29.0	
2	T. TAYLOR	1-31.4	1-31.3	
3	J. SURTEES	1-29.8		
4	L. BANDINI	1-33.4 (4)	1-31.0 (31)	1-30.4
5	G. HILL	1-31.2	1-30.4	
6	R. GINTHER	1-32.6	1-31.3	
7	E. PIETERSE	1-34.5		
8	J. BRABHAM	1-30.1	1-29.9	
9	D. GURNEY	1-30.2	1-30.1	
10	B. McLAREN	1-31.3		
11	A. MAGGS	1-32.4		
12	J. BONNIER	1-32.4		
13				
14	C. BEAUFORT	1-37.1	1-36.6	
15	E. DRIVER	1-38.7	1-37.?	

1963

Scoreboards

KEEPING IN TOUCH and knowing the score is essential for race fans. The circuit scoreboard may seem like old technology, but it's still the easiest way for racegoers to know what's going on in front of them. It can be confusing keeping in touch with who is running where in races in which a sudden rain shower sends drivers racing into the pits to change tyres, so a scoreboard is a helpful aid in letting all racegoers know who is out in front. Some scoreboards are also part of the furniture, such as at Indianapolis, where the huge, vertically stacked scoreboard is perhaps its defining landmark.

Early scoreboard technology had circuits using scoreboards like those you'd find at a cricket match, with scorers inserting car numbers into a rack. These were superseded by electronic displays but these too are becoming things of the past as circuits now run their own radio stations and race fans listen through small earpieces. The next step will be for the information on the timing screens in race control to be beamed to PDAs, but the loss of the traditional scoreboards will be a sad event.

Left: This photograph was shot at the 1963 South African GP at East London as driver Carel Godin de Beaufort (left) turns from the rudimentary blackboard

Right: The vertically stacked Indianapolis scoreboard has changed little over the years and is great as it can be seen from all points around the track

1932

Getting ready for the off

THE CLOCK IS TICKING, the pressure mounts and drivers need to keep their cool as the start of the race gets ever closer. However experienced a team or driver, the countdown to a grand prix is always a time of tension. The equipment, the circuits and the procedure have all changed since that first grand prix at Le Mans back in 1906, but the tension remains the same.

Nowadays, the countdown allows the cars to assemble on the grid as much as half an hour before the standard start time, with mechanics taking spare sets of tyres and even dry ice to put into the cars' radiators to keep the engine cool. Engineers plug in laptops to run a series of diagnostic tests to check the running condition of the engine and the tyres are wrapped in electric blankets to keep them at optimum temperature. Amid all this activity, the driver tries to keep calm and focused while appearing cheerful in the face of TV interviews, much like the bravado pupils display before taking an examination.

Left: Marcel Lehoux appears lost in thought as he sits all alone in his Bugatti before the start of the German GP in 1932, holding an umbrella to keep himself dry

Above: Michael Schumacher goes through his pre-set routine before the Japanese GP some 73 years later. The tension is just the same, only the details are different

1969

In the pit garage

IT'S THE MECHANICS' HOME FROM HOME, a place to keep the cars on race weekends. In dimensions, a modern-day pit garage may not be much larger than a triple garage, but it's packed with the tools and technology required to run a twenty-first century grand prix car. It's something that grand prix drivers up until the 1960s could only have dreamed of, as there were no pit garages then. They had to make do with something far more basic, with the tools to fettle their cars being brought to a pit counter and the cars worked on while sitting exposed to the elements in the pitlane.

Today's garages are fitted with all the lighting, electronic and hydraulic supplies that the teams require so that they can work on their cars 24 hours a day if they require, as they often do. Hoses and power leads can be pulled down from the ceiling for the mechanics' equipment as well as timing screens which drop down so that the drivers can check on exactly how they are faring against the opposition. In these days of subterfuge, it even allows the teams to keep some of their technical tricks secret.

Left: Facilities are all but uniform now, but they weren't always so. This underground car park was used as an overnight store for the cars for the 1969 Dutch GP

Right: Mark Webber protects his ears while his Red Bull mechanics perform an engine test in their fully-equipped pit garage in 2009

1922

In the pitlane

THE CARS GO SLOW, but the action is fast. That's life in the pitlane – that narrow strip of tarmac alongside the track where the cars receive orchestrated servicing and running repairs during the course of a grand prix. The most obvious difference between then and now is the fact that the early pitlanes were more like the hard shoulder of a motorway and were not separated from the start/finish straight by a pitwall. These didn't arrive until the 1960s. Separating the pitlane was an obvious thing to do in the name of safety as the thought of a car crashing at racing speed into those working on their cars doesn't bear thinking about.

The other difference is the number of people working on each car as the early racers used to hop out, along with their riding mechanic, to do the work themselves. In the twenty-first century, more than a dozen highly trained mechanics follow a synchronized and much-rehearsed procedure. Refuelling, along with changing all four tyres, can be done in as little as six seconds.

Left: Long before the pitlane was separated from the track by a wall, Giulio Foresti works on his Ballot in the French GP. Note the spare wheels behind him

Right: With ample space to perform their mid-race pit stop duties in relative safety in 2005, Renault's pit crew have no idea how fortunate they are

1968

The build-up

THE ACTION BEFORE THE ACTION is the best way to describe pre-race entertainment. It's a way of entertaining the spectators and building the anticipation for the racing that will follow, setting the start procedure in motion with a blaze of colour and noise.

Pre-race entertainment in the early twentieth century tended to consist of a marching band, but by the 1960s grands prix across the globe started to compete with each other to see who could put on the most outlandish show, often bringing the air force or a stunt pilot in for an air display. One year a Hawker Harrier jump jet, having finished its manoeuvres, parked on the infield, which suddenly didn't seem such a good idea when it was nearly hit by an errant car...

Pre-race entertainment is standardized with the presentation of the national flag and the arrival of the grid girls, but a bit more rock and roll might be appreciated.

Right: With every passing year in the 1960s, pre-race entertainment became more outlandish. Here, a man with a jetpack thrills the crowds at Brands Hatch

Far right: Some pre-race parades are harder to comprehend than others, such as this one at the 2005 Chinese GP, but they're bright and entertaining

1961

Ligging

SOMETIMES A SANDWICH JUST WON'T DO when you attend a grand prix. Some days, a punnet of *frites mayonnaise* is perfect when standing in the Ardennes forest watching cars flash by on the majestic Spa-Francorchamps. When entertaining guests, however, Cordon Bleu cooking is now a must and this explains the rise and rise of the multi-million-dollar Paddock Club.

The Paddock Club is a world within a world, a clutch of luxury, air-conditioned marquees with hot and cold drinks running all day and its own grandstand nearby. It's corporate and it doesn't come cheap, but the luxury is undeniable. This is important, not to the petrol-head race fan, but to the teams' sponsors and their guests and it's a far cry from the days up until the 1970s when a local restaurant would simply deliver a few trays of food to a team's garage or the team's hierarchy would drive out to lunch at a local hostelry.

Left: The atmosphere in the paddock for the 1961 French GP at a sunny Reims is freeform and fun, but you had to buy drinks or bring your own

Right: The paddock is now an exclusive setting. Sir Jackie Stewart entertains the written media on behalf of Williams sponsor, the Royal Bank of Scotland

1960

Transporters

TAILOR-MADE TRUCKS are the favoured way of transporting grand prix cars to the tracks. Emphasizing the changing of the parameters, each team today takes three transporters to a grand prix, each one bigger than the single transporter that teams like Ferrari would use in the 1950s and 1960s. Bear in mind, too, that Ferrari would enter as many as four cars in a grand prix back then...

Today's race transporters are the size of a juggernaut, liveried in the teams' colours and kept resplendent at all times. On the road they are rolling billboards for the teams, in the paddock the nerve centre of their weekend's activity. One transporter will carry the cars, another the spare parts plus workshop equipment and the third the engines. With so many tools and so much equipment to be carried, not an inch of space is wasted. Transporters also house offices for the engineers and several teams have these on an extra deck that is raised hydraulically above the roofline of the transporter. It's small wonder that they cost more than £1 million each.

Right: Looking for all the world like a converted coach, which it was, the Ferrari transporter arrives at Zandvoort for the Dutch GP with its cars exposed

Far right: This 2009 Brawn GP transporter extends upwards when parked, with its upper deck rising up on hydraulics to double its size, even joining on to the sister transporter at upper storey level

1958

Motorhomes

FIFTY YEARS AGO THEY DIDN'T EXIST, yet now team motorhomes can be larger than a four-bedroomed house. Yes, inflation in this department is almost greater than any other facet of the grand prix world. Put simply, a motorhome is a sanctuary for the team's top management and drivers to escape from the elements and the attention of the public.

Early-day drivers had nowhere to hide and then latter-day ones went for a snooze underneath their pit counter or in their hire car. But the American-style motorhome arrived in the 1970s. As soon as one team had one, the rest had to follow. They grew bigger and flashier with every passing year. By the 1990s, these were replaced by coach-sized vehicles with a massive awning under which the team would eat. McLaren even had a window in theirs that could be turned into a television screen. But that is now so yesterday, as McLaren introduced a portable building in 2002 that could be taken and assembled at each track, with a central atrium as its heart and offices and catering facilities arranged around its flanks.

Left: This was as close as Tony Brooks got to a motorhome in the 1950s as he accepts a cup of tea from the tail of the Ferodo estate car at Zandvoort

Right: The Red Bull Energy Station – considerably larger than many family houses – took paddock hospitality on to even greater levels in 2005

Four

Petrolheads & Pitbabes

Right: Things were done differently in the 1960s: this is Jim Clark and his Lotus 25 going for a lap of honour on a flatbed trailer after winning the 1963 British GP

1958

Women racers

IT'S STILL A MAN'S WORLD since Formula One started, an all-male bastion that has never been conquered by a woman racing driver. That's not to say that a few haven't tried. As yet, however, none have shone on the grand prix scene.

There have been lady racers from the 1920s onwards, with Czech Elizabeth Junek leading the way in taking on the men in the lengthy races of the day, finishing fourth overall and first in class in the 1927 German GP. Several ladies drove with courage on the banking at Brooklands. However, it was not until 1958 that Maria Teresa de Fillipis became the first woman to try and qualify for a World Championship grand prix, making it at her second attempt in her privately entered Maserati. Divina Galica attempted to follow suit in the 1970s, but never made the cut in either a Surtees or a Hesketh and Desire Wilson – winner of a non-championship F1 race at Brands Hatch – also missed out in a Williams in 1980. The last woman racer to try was Giovanna Amati in 1992. She too ended up just short of the target for the fast-declining Brabham team, making way for Damon Hill to break into Formula One and go on to become World Champion.

Right: Maria Teresa de Fillipis failed in her first attempt to qualify at Monaco in 1958, but went on to make three grand prix starts

Far right: It was only a test, but Katherine Legge's outing in a Minardi in 2005 made her the first woman to drive a grand prix car for 13 years

Left: It's all eyes at the 1960 Italian GP as one of a pair of race officials fails in his attempt not to notice a local beauty parading on the grid

Right: Grid girls have official, orchestrated roles to play, marking where a driver must stop on the grid

1960

Glamour pusses

GRID GIRLS ADD GLAMOUR to the proceedings of a grand prix. It may be sexist, but they represent a colourful sideshow to the racing, albeit an orchestrated one and television directors and magazine editors always carry shots of them.

In the days before the paddock was off limits to anyone without the correct official pass, pretty girls would flock in, hoping to catch the eye of the visiting heroes. They were almost as much a part of the scene as the drivers and some knew that this was their chance to be spotted and perhaps propelled into a world of modelling or even film. So their clothes became ever skimpier and teams worked out the value of employing a model or two to drape over the car for a photo-shoot to ensure their sponsors receive maximum coverage.

1950

Royalty

BY ROYAL APPOINTMENT is a powerful recommendation and the first-ever round of the World Championship at Silverstone in 1950 received just that. The then Queen Elizabeth was guest of honour, adding powerful patronage to an event that was seen as a step forward in the wake of World War Two.

Every country hosting a grand prix wants the support of their royal family and, most famously, Monaco has this at each and every grand prix with Prince Albert taking over in 2005 after the death of his father, Prince Rainier. King Juan Carlos of Spain is another motorsport fan. Likewise, the Emir of Bahrain made a point of attending his country's first grand prix.

Some royals go a step further and the Princess Royal's son, Peter Phillips, has worked for the sponsorship divisions of both Jaguar Racing and Williams, whereas his cousin, Prince Andrew, has attended grands prix on behalf of the Department of Trade and Industry, promoting the interests of British companies involved in the sport.

Right: The first-ever round of the World Championship, the British GP in 1950, is attended by the then Queen Elizabeth, later the Queen Mother

Far right: These days, royalty work in the sport: the Queen's grandson, Peter Phillips, catches up with his uncle, Prince Andrew, at the 2005 Bahrain GP

1966

Celebrities

THE CAMERAS ARE THERE, which encourages celebrity attendance, but quite a few celebrities love racing anyway. Perhaps chief among these was Beatle George Harrison, who attended as many grands prix as possible in the 1970s after being introduced to the sport as a child at the Aintree circuit just outside his native Liverpool. But if he was on the grid before the start, he was seeking out his friends among the drivers, rather than wanting to be photographed by the press.

Actors Michael Douglas and Nicholas Cage are fans as well, while Sylvester Stallone spent a year or two at races in preparation for a film he never made. Harrison was by no means the only visitor from the music world. Singer Jamiroquai is a serious petrolhead who loves the sport as much for the nuts and bolts of the cars and the intricacies of the racing as for the posturing on the grid.

Left: Monaco attracts celebrities like no other race, as shown by actor Peter Sellers and model wife Britt Ekland talking to Graham Hill and Jackie Stewart

Right: Fallen boxing world champion Mike Tyson looks to restore his profile at the 2005 Turkish GP with Bernie Ecclestone as his guide

Above: It's the 1968 Italian GP and a member of the *tifosi* peers into a Rolls-Royce entering the Monza paddock in the hope of spotting one of their heroes

Right: The closest Britain came to the *tifosi*'s fanaticism was in the early 1990s when Nigel Mansell's winning form creates 'Mansell-mania' and, sadly, track invasions

Trackside passion

IF IT'S RED, THEN CHEER, if it's not, then jeer: this is the attitude of the *tifosi*, the oft one-eyed fans of the Ferrari team. This may sound overly jingoistic, but you can't fault them for passion. If anything, you can only fault them for excess emotional involvement.

They have enjoyed some incredible years with Michael Schumacher since he returned the team to winning ways in 1998, but their support is consistently partisan. There were times in the 1980s when Ferrari was not so dominant that they would turn tail and leave mid-race if both of their beloved red cars retired.

The closest thing to the passion demonstrated by the *tifosi* was the explosion of 'Mansell-mania' in the late 1980s when Nigel Mansell started performing heroics for Williams. He was the 'British Bulldog', always fast and 100 per cent committed and never less than dramatic. He brought hordes of new fans to the sport, although the downside was that thousands became so over-excited when 'our Nige' won at Silverstone that they invaded the track before the final lap was complete.

1937

Showing your colours

DRESSING THE PART is as important to the fans as it is to the drivers. It's not just a way of keeping out the cold or shading oneself from the sun according to the weather conditions, but it's also a way of showing your tribal loyalty to the team of your choice. Many a fan in their fifities still has a black and gold JPS Lotus jacket at the back of their wardrobe, much as those in their thirties may have a Canon Williams one.

It was very different before teams became branded. Photographs from the 1920s and 1930s show how all fans wore a uniform, but that uniform was simply a coat, a hat and a scarf. Nowadays, it's easier to spot which section of the grandstand is supporting which team – although you can guarantee one thing and this is that the majority will be in red, as Ferrari remains the pick of the bunch in every country visited.

Left: The uniform is, well, uniform at Donington Park in 1937 with so many of the crowd wearing a hat and a scarf. Branded clothing is another 30 years away

Right: No nation dresses up as much as the Japanese. They're open to all, even though Michael Schumacher's form has made Ferrari their favourite

1960

Racing's reliables

THE LIFEBLOOD OF THE SPORT are the fans and they want to get as close to the cars, drivers and action as possible. Access to the cars and drivers has unfortunately become ever more difficult in the past 20 years as the paddock behind the pits is fenced off with access only for those with the correct pass. This means acquiring an autograph from a hero is now much trickier, something that is a huge shame and something that would have been quite unthinkable in the 1950s or 1960s.

To many, lurking outside the hotels where the teams are staying is now the only option to steal a word or offer encouragement. Many dig deep into their pockets to pay for a chance to go on a pit walkabout simply to get a glance at the cars, the equipment and, hopefully, a driver or two. With this desired access denied them, many fans would like to make a protest by not attending the races, but the lure of the race action remains far too strong. However, a message to the powers that be: ignore the fans at your peril.

Right: When paddock access was open to all, children such as these could get close to their heroes. Here Innes Ireland does the honours

Far right: Fans of grand prix racing always like to have a voice, especially when they feel that politics is starting to take over from the sport that they love

Five

The Rest of the Crew

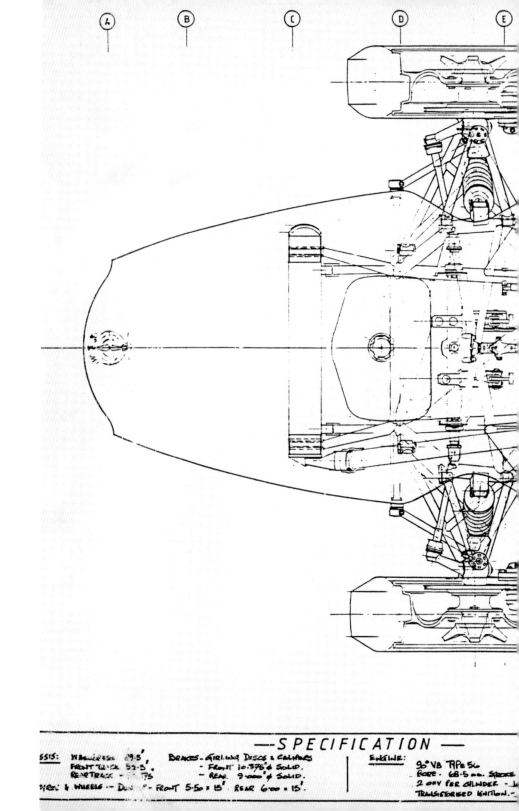

Right: In the days before computers, cars were drawn by hand. This is the blueprint of the BRM P57 with which Graham Hill won the 1962 crown

—SPECIFICATION—

SSIS: WHEELBASE 89.5',
FRONT TRACK 52.5,
REAR TRACK 53.75

BRAKES - GIRLING DISCS & CALIPERS
- FRONT 10.375'ø SOLID.
- REAR. 9.000'ø SOLID.

ENGINE: 90° V8 TYPE 56
BORE. 68.5 mm. STROKE
2 OHV PER CYLINDER
TRANSISTORISED IGNITION.

TYRES & WHEELS - DUN'P - FRONT 5.50 x 15' REAR 6.00 x 15'.

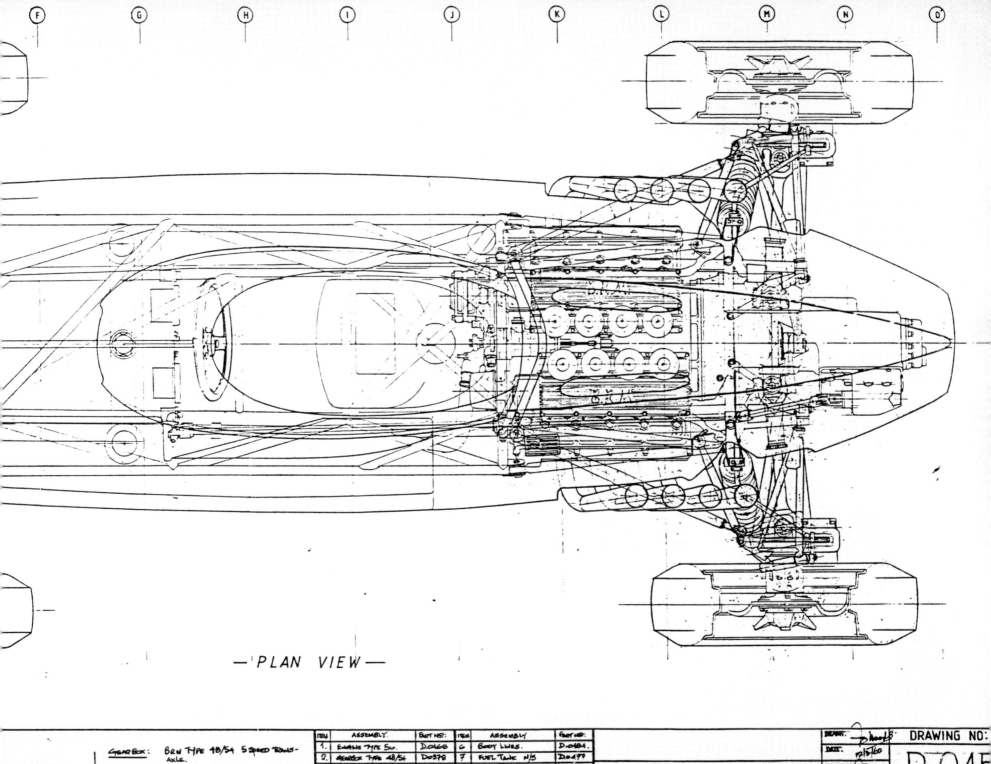

— PLAN VIEW —

Bernie Ecclestone

HE'S THE ULTIMATE DEAL-MAKER and now one of the richest men in the world. He dealt so successfully in cars and motorbikes in his twenties that he was able to buy the Connaught team and make his own attempt to qualify for a grand prix in 1958 after a brief career in Formula Three. He failed to make the cut, but this was not the last heard of Bernie Ecclestone. Indeed, far from it...

Ecclestone was already managing a driver, Stuart Lewis-Evans, but he was killed and it was not until the late 1960s that he returned, managing the burgeoning career of Jochen Rindt. Sadly, he, too, perished in action. Undaunted, Ecclestone turned to team ownership, buying the Brabham team in 1972, running it until the end of 1987 and collecting two drivers' titles courtesy of Nelson Piquet in 1981 and 1983. During that time, Ecclestone also became the front man for the teams in their perennial battle against the race promoters, leading their fight for better start money. By far the best businessman among the team chiefs, he effectively took control of their promotional rights and this made him one of the world's wealthiest men.

Left: At the United States GP in 2005, Bernie Ecclestone surveys his fiefdom, ensuring that the show is as professional as he wants it to be

Far left: Life was simpler for Bernie when he *only* had to run Brabham. Bernie (right) talks shop with Gordon Murray and Carlos Reutemann at the 1975 Belgian GP

1955

The bigshots

CALLING ALL THE SHOTS is the old approach of the team boss. Some of the most successful grand prix team bosses have been autocrats, managers who brooked no opinion other than their own. Certainly, this is a management style that has all but disappeared today, yet things were very different until as late as the 1960s. It was done the way the team chief suggested or not at all.

Two of the best-known grand prix autocrats were Mercedes-Benz sporting manager Alfred Neubauer and Ferrari founder Enzo Ferrari, men who learned their art before World War Two. The good thing about them was that, whether right or wrong, no-one could say that they didn't know where their team boss stood on any matter. The team came first and the drivers very much second, especially as far as Ferrari was concerned. Louis Stanley of BRM was another cut from the same cloth.

Left: Perhaps the most fearsome and autocratic of all: Mercedes-Benz sporting boss Alfred Neubauer oversees the action at the British GP at Aintree

Right: Enzo Ferrari was the only other boss who could match Neubauer for silent admonition. The difference was that Enzo was answerable to no-one

1963

Driving them on

MENTOR AND PUPIL is a good way to describe the relationship between certain team managers and their star drivers. These team chiefs can be autocratic as well, but their predominant style is to nurture their drivers, not only to coax the best out of them, but to ensure that they don't feel tempted to join a rival team.

One of the earliest examples of a team boss as friend as well as manager was Lotus chief Colin Chapman with Jim Clark in the early 1960s, when the combination of technical and driving genius put them in a class of their own. That they were of similar age helped, as further shown by Frank Williams and Patrick Head who have never been as close to any of their drivers as they were to their contemporary Alan Jones in the early 1980s.

Flavio Briatore is markedly older than Renault's first World Champion Fernando Alonso, but he has built a friendship based on similar interests and by inviting Alonso to stay at his Kenyan beach hideaway. For all their fun, however, this still didn't stop Alonso from signing for McLaren without telling him.

Right: Lotus chief Colin Chapman and his ace Jim Clark are deep in thought as they discuss chassis set-up before a run-out in practice at Zandvoort

Far right: Even away from the circuits, Renault boss Flavio Briatore likes to keep his drivers close. Here, he trains with Trulli and Alonso in Kenya in 2001

1957

Patriots

THEY LOVE THEIR COUNTRIES. These rich patriots are more than happy to put their money where their hearts are and invest their fortunes in the pursuit of national glory. This had more cachet up until the late 1960s, when teams ran in their national racing colours.

Tony Vandervell is one such patriot. He invested in BRM's long-winded and largely flawed attempts to hoist the Union flag on the grand prix scene, but became tired when they perpetually missed the target. So, what did he do? Ran his own programme, of course. His Vanwall team was far more successful thanks to Stirling Moss and Tony Brooks winning the inaugural constructors' title in 1958. Also armed with money and ambition, Lord Hesketh had similar dreams in the early 1970s, with the insouciant charger James Hunt at the wheel of his red, white and blue cars with their teddy bear mascot. Hunt toppled Niki Lauda and Ferrari in the 1975 Dutch Grand Prix, but then the cost of taking on the giants spiralled too high for an individual to play.

Left: Tony Vandervell was determined his team would make Britain winners. He celebrates here with Tony Brooks and Stirling Moss after the British GP

Right: Lord Hesketh, James Hunt, 'Bubbles' Horsley and Harvey Postlethwaite are happy at Zandvoort, knowing not that Hunt would deliver their first win

1971

Talent spotters

KEEPING AN EYE ON YOUNG TALENT. Team bosses watch the upcoming stars in the junior formulae as it's the best way to snap up the services of the stars of tomorrow. This is especially true of those bosses who want to place them on a long-term management deal out of which they will make a tidy sum when these up-and-coming aces hit the big time. Take the most successful of all, Willi Weber, who had the vision, not to say good fortune, to spot the speed of a young Michael Schumacher and snap him up on a ten per cent management deal. Ten per cent of $50million, yearly, can be more than a little useful.

Ken Tyrrell became famed for spotting the stars of the future and Jackie Stewart was the perfect advertisement of this. Eddie Jordan is always on the look-out, helped by his background in Formula Three and Formula 3000, and he picked out the likes of Jean Alesi, even giving Michael Schumacher his grand prix debut in 1991, before the German was snatched by Benetton. However, the team chief who puts the most effort into this is Ron Dennis whose annual McLaren *Autosport* BRDC Young Driver scheme helped David Coulthard and Jenson Button to the top.

Left: Willi Weber (arms crossed) watches on as his charge Michael Schumacher larks around before making his F1 debut at Spa-Francorchamps in 1991

Far left: Ken Tyrrell was long acknowledged as a talent spotter and he ran Jackie Stewart in Formula Three before they rejoined forces in F1 four years later

1967

Unsung heroes

RACING WOULDN'T HAPPEN WITHOUT the often invisible race officials. When people think of the key individuals that make grand prix racing tick, they generally list the drivers, team bosses, engineers and mechanics. It's easy to overlook the involvement of the army of race officials, a block of individuals without whom there would be no racing at all.

These include everyone from the person who triggers the lights to start the race to the unpaid marshals who line the circuits to ensure the safety of the drivers and clear up the wreckage created by accidents. The ones at the top of the tree who get to wear the smartest blazers are the race stewards, whose role is to ensure that every grand prix is run according to the rule book. They have the power to fine any driver or team who transgresses these rules in a quest for an unfair advantage. They may be invisible to those watching a race, but their power is felt everywhere.

Right: Having the right credentials means these individuals are allowed to stand dangerously close to flying cars to man a speed trap at Silverstone in 1967

Far right: All officials are better clothed for their particular jobs these days. Here's a firesuited flag marshal in action at the 2005 Spanish GP

147

1966

Designers

THESE ARE THE BRAINBOXES who think in three dimensions and who can visualize how best to translate the latest set of technical regulations into a winning grand prix car. In the early days, draughtsmen would work together at the drawing board to shape the great racers from Alfa Romeo, Auto Union, Bugatti and Mercedes-Benz. Later, sharp-witted individuals such as Lotus founder Colin Chapman would famously take a less measured approach in the 1960s, jotting down his latest thoughts on the back of a cigarette packet as he bounced from one task to another.

Then dawned the age of the computer and the specialist designer who is free to work solely in concept, rather than seeing the job through from outset to reality. No longer was everything sketched and then handed to production engineers to turn into reality. The designers' box of tricks became all the more potent from the 1980s onwards, with three-dimensional modelling enabling an idea to be checked from all angles, even for imaginary airflow, thus heading off the design bloopers of old that cost so much time and money to correct.

Left: Mauro Forghieri was Ferrari's brains in the 1960s and 1970s. Here, the Italian designer oversees the team's cars in a garage at the French GP

Right: Adrian Newey has led the way for the past two decades and he never stops jotting notes onto his notepad. This is him with McLaren in 1999

1961
Engineers

WITH A TWEAK, A NIP AND A TUCK a race engineer can make all the difference to the handling of a car, helping his driver find those vital fractions of a second that transform a mediocre qualifying lap into a great one. They are not the progenitors of the design ideas, but they are the ones who massage a car towards its potential.

Working with suspension, aerodynamic body parts and tyres, they can transform how a car will handle and adapt it to the prevailing weather, wind and track conditions, while tailoring it according to a specific driver's style. Better still, they'll iron out any design shortfalls and have a clear development programme that will bring the car on through the season. The best of today's engineers do more than that, however, as they are also managers who oversee a division of staff. Ferrari's Ross Brawn and Renault's Pat Symonds stand out as this sort of engineer, following in the footsteps of John Cooper in the 1950s and designer/engineer Patrick Head from the 1980s.

Right: John Cooper was one of the forerunners of British engineering excellence who turned the sport on its head. He's shown on the look-out at Zandvoort

Far right: Mike Gascoyne is the man whose engineering brain turned Toyota into a front-running team. He chats here with Ralf Schumacher in 2005

1937

Mechanics

RACING MECHANICS WANT MORE than the easy life: simply working in the local garage close to home wouldn't be for them. No, in order to pursue their dream, grand prix mechanics are prepared to travel the world and work incredibly long hours, often for little more pay than they would receive at the local garage. The glory, camaraderie and glamour of travel encourage them.

The role of mechanic has changed, however. At the start of grand prix racing all cars carried a riding mechanic, someone to repair the car when it faltered on those early road circuits with ultra-long laps. But they were soon dispensed with, due to reasons of weight and any problems were tended to by trained mechanics in the pits. Yet pit stops were slow back then and now their role has changed out of all recognition with planned pitstops for fuel and a new set of tyres, where the ability to keep cool and not make a slip-up is essential and speed is as important as it is out on the track. Thriving on little sleep and enormous pressure is now a must.

Above: The Williams refuelling crew of 2005 are primed and ready, their working environment a world apart from their forerunners'

Left: There's plenty to do, but few hands to the pumps at the 1937 Donington GP. Note, too, how rudimentary the tools are

1961
Technical advances

CUTTING-EDGE TECHNOLOGY HAS ALWAYS GONE hand in hand with grand prix racing. However, it's not just in car, engine and tyre technology that progress has been made, but in the tools of the trade as well. A hammer was once the main weapon of choice for solving mid-race mechanical failures, wielded of course by the riding mechanic. But the arrival of specialist mechanics in the 1920s brought an upgrade on the tools front.

Everything was still solid-state until the 1960s, however. As with chassis design, the advent of computers changed all this. First of all, laptops attached in the pits performed an instant diagnosis of the engine's heartbeat. Then, in the 1980s, telemetry allowed teams to monitor these vital functions even as the cars circled the track. Better still, they then beamed them back to base by satellite for extra analysis. How a driver of the 1930s or even the 1970s would marvel at being handed a print-out illustrating how much throttle, brake and steering application they had at any point around a lap.

Left: It was state of the art then, but Ferrari's charge checker looks now like a museum piece. No wonder then that a visual check appeals more to the mechanics

Right: By the late 1990s, drivers were expected to analyse every aspect of their car's performance with their engineers. This is Mika Hakkinen looking serious

1952
Liveries

THINK RED AND YOU THINK FERRARI, but how many fans in 2006 know that it's also Italy's national racing colour? In the early days of last century, the nationalities of cars were made plain to onlookers by their colour scheme as national honour was the key. It was blue for France, silver for Germany, dark green for Great Britain, white with blue stripes for the USA and orange for Holland.

However, the arrival of commercial sponsorship brought an end to this habit and individual team liveries became the norm. Imagine how complicated it would be to identify the cars in the thick of race action today if all the cars run out of headquarters in Britain were painted dark green, as that would include the cars from seven of the 11 teams, namely McLaren, Williams, Renault, Honda Racing, Red Bull Racing, Midland F1 and Super Aguri Racing. Perhaps it is best, therefore, that teams are identified by the colours of their sponsors, although the power of patriotism shouldn't be underestimated.

Right: National colours were the order of the day in the 1950s. Rudolf Fischer's Ferrari 500 is red with a white stripe, for Switzerland, in his home grand prix

Far right: The Warsteiner brewery sponsored Arrows in 1979, but few companies can afford to have an entire car in their livery in the 21st century

1968

Sponsorship

MOTOR RACING WILL ALWAYS BE EXPENSIVE. It's hardly surprising then that money is required to ensure that a team can offer its drivers the best equipment. In the early days of racing, the teams were fielded directly by the motor manufacturers with road car sales financing the racing. However, it was the advent of specialist racing teams in the 1950s that led to the need for money to be raised directly. Many teams had wealthy patrons and their input was bolstered by free tyres and lubricants whose payback was a discreet sticker low on the car's flanks.

Costs continued to rise, however. The face of grand prix racing changed for ever at the start of 1968 when the dark green Lotus cars with their yellow nose bands were repainted in red, white and gold, with the emblems of Gold Leaf tobacco adorning their every surface. Sponsorship had arrived and every team followed suit. It upset the purists, but some of the best liveries are fabulously attractive, although few will rival the black with gold keystripes of the John Player Lotus team of the 1970s.

Right: Lotus sets the ball rolling in F1 sponsorship with their Gold Leaf livery. Here, Graham Hill and Jackie Oliver line up on the front row at Brands Hatch

Far right: Where tobacco sponsorship was banned, teams ran look-alike liveries, such as Damon Hill's Buzzing Hornets (Benson & Hedges) Jordan in 1998

1959

Gift of the gab

TALKING FAST AND THINKING FASTER is the role of the commentator. Some circuits offer a view of much of their lap, enabling spectators to keep abreast of the action. However, the circuit commentator is key to the entertainment, building up the excitement of the occasion through the PA system and calling the race from their superior viewpoint, often with as many as three co-commentators spread around the circuit.

In the early days, the commentators saw little more than the spectators, but the advent of television meant they finally caught 100 per cent of the action and could call the race accordingly. Electronic timing means that a glance at a monitor also confirms the positions of the drivers, the intervals between them and their lap times. Once motor racing became really popular, circuit commentators were joined by television commentators who quickly became household names. Murray Walker is the most famous of all, as popular for his occasional gaffes as for his rampant enthusiasm.

Left: With this deerstalker hat and tweed jacket, it could only be 1950s' racer-turned-commentator John Bolster set to entertain at Goodwood

Right: The most famous television commentator of all time, the ever-enthusiastic Murray Walker, interviews his good friend Damon Hill in the 1990s

Above: If you're talking exposure, it's safe to say that this posse of lens men beyond the meagre barrier are incredibly over-exposed as they catch the action on the climb to Massenet at Monaco in 1971

Right: Putting a crash barrier between the photographers and the cars, as shown here at the 2005 Hungarian GP, is a clear step forward, but their limited access means they often shoot as a pack

1971

Photographers

FAST CARS, CAMERAS AND ACTION. To many grand prix fans, this is the dream job, after being the driver of course. A photographer on the grand prix beat is seen as wildly glamorous and exciting. However, the job is not as glamorous as many think and the best exponents are true craftsmen consistently trying to dream up original shots, something that is increasingly tricky as they are corralled into designated zones.

They are envious of the greater freedom of their predecessors, but the licence to stand where they like meant photographers in the past were often in danger of being hit by the cars. Today, photographers are protected from the cars and debris by safety fences, but these fences are their bane as well. The most remarkable improvement is in the calibre of their equipment, with their largest lenses more than making up for the fact that they've been pushed back from standing right on the edge of the track.

Six

Life in the Fast Lane

Right: The cars were released one at a time
in the early days. Georges Boillot (5) and Rene
Champoiseau (6) line up for the 1914 French GP

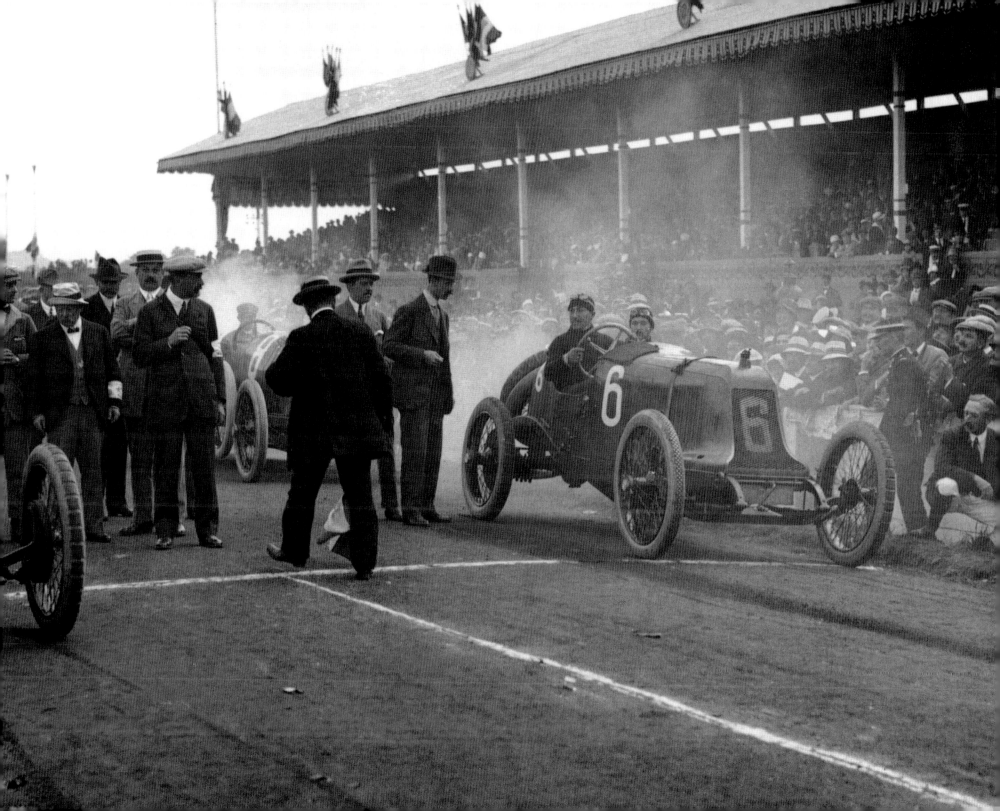

1932

Race starts

READY, STEADY, GO might be the accepted way of starting a running race at school, but in keeping with its long-running traditions, grand prix racing predictably demands something a little more random, so the start of the race – always the best point for a driver to overtake another and therefore of vital importance – is a lottery.

For the first half century and more, a grand prix got under way with the most highly ranked race official waving the national flag from a position just ahead of the grid, often while standing on the track. However, this was upgraded with the advent of electronic starting lights on a gantry ahead of the grid.

The most recent version is for drivers to watch a row of five red lights being illuminated one at a time. Then, when all five are lit, they must wait, their cars at a standstill, for them all to go out, something that can happen between 4 and 7 seconds after that. If they anticipate this prematurely, they will be hit with a time penalty.

Above: Jenson Button leads away from pole to open the 2009 season, getting his Brawn into Melbourne's Turn 1 ahead of Sebastian Vettel, Nico Rosberg and Kimi Raikkonen

Left: It's 'Williams' (Bugatti), Philippe Etancelin (Alfa Romeo) and Amedeo Ruggeri (Maserati) to the fore as they wait for the flag to drop to signal the start at Monaco in 1932

1906

Pit stops

LESS HASTE MORE SPEED is a maxim that holds true when it comes to pit stops. Clearly, the aim is – and always has been – to get the car back out onto the track again as soon as possible, but a crossthreaded wheel nut can spell disaster in a sport in which a second means the difference between success and failure. Time and again, members of the pit crew have pushed just that fraction too hard and ruined the driver's whole afternoon of work.

There was a period during the twentieth century when pit stops were only employed to change a car onto wet-weather tyres if it rained or vice versa. However, Brabham decided to introduce refuelling again in the early 1980s as they reckoned the time gained by sending a car out to start the race with the weight advantage of a half tank of fuel was worth the time taken to pit, add the other half tank of fuel and rejoin. Mid-race tyre changes became popular later, some teams even changing tyres as many as three times in a grand prix so that they could run on fresh, sticky tyres with a tiny load of fuel.

Left: Philippe Tavenaux attends to his Gregoire in that first-ever grand prix, held at Le Mans in 1906. Note the three spare tyres behind the driver's seat

Right: At the 2005 French GP, it's totally different as the Williams crew runs through its preordained steps to supply Nick Heidfeld with a new set of tyres

1982
Driver rescue

IF A DRIVER IS HURT, extreme care is needed to remove him from a crashed car. In the early days of grand prix racing, drivers were often thrown clear of the car because no seatbelts were worn. However, once seatbelts were adopted and cars were fitted with roll-over hoops, they would often be contained within their cockpits, even after an inversion, but sometimes with injuries – especially in the early 1980s when drivers' feet were ahead of the front axle. With fuel tanks harder to puncture, fire was less of a risk and there was less need to get the driver out of the car as fast as possible.

The biggest risk when yanking a driver out of a car by the handles on the shoulders of their race overalls is that any spinal injury might be aggravated. Instead, in the 1990s, a tray-style splint was introduced to slide behind the driver's back before they were removed. However, the most important element in driver extrication is the training of marshals and the introduction of the HANS (head and neck safety) device. This came in at the start of the twenty-first century and restricts the overextension of a drivers' neck – whiplash – in an impact

Left: Marshals arrive to extract Rene Arnoux from his Renault as it sits atop the tyre wall and crash barrier at Tarzan corner in the 1982 Dutch GP

Right: There are many more rescue vehicles in evidence at the 2005 US GP where Ralf Schumacher hit the wall in the same spot as in 2004

1968

In the wet

IT'S KNOWN AS AQUAPLANING. When driving through rain on the track the steering can go light and a driver finds he is no longer in control of his car. It can happen to anyone, at any time, but the true greats of grand prix racing display skills in knowing how hard to push and how to bring their car back under control should it go light after hitting an unexpected stream across the track.

Gilles Villeneuve was acknowledged as a superstar in the wet, lapping 11 seconds faster than anyone else in a soaking practice session at Watkins Glen in 1979, but even he failed to produce a drive as stunning as Jackie Stewart's on the treacherous-in-the-dry, lethal-in-the-wet Nurburgring Nordschleife in 1968 when, with fog adding to the hellish conditions, he managed to win by more than four minutes. Displaying equal mastery of the wet, Ayrton Senna matched his expertise in dry conditions with an astonishing charge from fifth place to first in the course of the opening lap of the 1993 Grand Prix of Europe at Donington Park.

Above: There was a deluge at the 1991 Australian GP that left the drivers either blinded, aquaplaning or both. Ayrton Senna, shown here leading, was declared the winner when it stopped early

Left: The Nurburgring Nordschleife is difficult in any circumstances. In rain like this in 1968, it was lethal, but Jackie Stewart mastered it in his Matra and won by more than four minutes...

1959

Heat that hurts

EXTREME HEAT IS UNPLEASANT. Have you ever been too hot to think or focus? You long to cool down immediately. Pity the grand prix driver in this predicament who has to press on with the next hour or so of the race. Extreme heat is an occasional part of racing for which little can be done, especially as grands prix are now being held in hotter locations such as Bahrain and Malaysia.

Driving is physical, even in cool conditions, so imagine what it must be like on days when the air temperature is in the 100s and the heat in the cockpit feels unbearable even through three-piece overalls. With no exposed flesh, there's no way for drivers to lose heat and they can sweat away as much as 2kg during a race. At least drivers today have dieticians who ensure that the mix in their drink bottle keeps adding the salts their body is leaking and so stave off cramp. Drivers of yesteryear had no such luxuries, but merely raced in short-sleeved shirts to keep them cool.

Left: Jack Brabham collapses in exhaustion after pushing his car to the finish in the 1959 US GP, but it was enough to help him to his first world title

Right: The thermometer says it all at the 2005 Malaysian GP: it's 117° Fahrenheit in the shade, to say nothing of the humidity

1939

Up in flames

FIRES USED TO BE THE DRIVERS' WORST FEAR, but, thankfully, they're considerably less dangerous now that drivers are clad head to toe in fireproof clothing. Amazingly, up to the 1950s, drivers wanted to be thrown clear of their crashed cars, risking broken limbs or worse to avoid being trapped in a flaming car.

Spilled fuel can often trigger a conflagration. To be precise, it's spilled fuel coming into contact with a hot engine or exhaust, as with the accident that claimed the life of Roger Williamson in the 1973 Dutch Grand Prix when his car inverted.

The introduction of deformable bag tanks in place of the rigid, metal-encased fuel tanks of old was a mammoth leap forward, but even better are lock-off valves that close should the bag tank become separated from the engine.

For all this, the return of refuelling pitstops made fires more likely again and Jos Verstappen could have been incinerated at the 1994 German Grand Prix. Eddie Irvine also survived a flash fire in the 1995 Belgian Grand Prix.

Above: Before fuel tanks were protected, cars often burst into flame on impact, transforming a minor accident into a major one. Dick Seaman died in this pyre at the 1939 Belgian GP

Right: Jos Verstappen was trapped in his car during this inferno, but he and his Benetton mechanics escaped with minor burns from this flash fire during a pit stop in the 1994 German GP

1973

The safety car

SOME CURSE ITS ARRIVAL, but there's no doubting that the introduction of the safety car has been a major contributor to driver safety. The idea is that it is deployed to slot into the race order ahead of the leader whenever there is a potentially dangerous situation on the circuit, such as a crashed car lying near the racing line which means the cars need to be slowed while it is cleared. The safety car must be driven by a capable driver, as the field can't afford to be slowed too much or their tyre temperatures will drop below their operating window.

The Americans had long used safety cars in their racing, but it wasn't until the Canadian GP in 1973 that one was first scrambled into action in a World Championship grand prix. Brought out after Jody Scheckter clashed with Francois Cevert, it appeared not to pick up the race leader but a backmarker, allowing McLaren's Peter Revson to gain almost a lap and go on to win from Lotus's Emerson Fittipaldi who was left perplexed as he said he hadn't been overtaken. Fortunately, matters have improved since then.

Above: The 1997 Belgian GP was the first to be started behind the safety car, on this occasion due to a treacherously wet track after a sudden downpour. Jacques Villeneuve's Williams follows in its wake

Left: The first time that a safety car was deployed was at the Canadian GP of 1973. The trouble was that it came out in front of a driver who wasn't leading the race, confusing matters more than a little

181

1952

Lines of communication

KEEPING THE DRIVER INFORMED AT ALL TIMES is crucial. They need to know who is gaining on them or whether they're pulling clear and can afford to back off in order to spare their engine, transmission and tyres. A glance ahead or in their mirrors simply doesn't keep them in the picture sufficiently well, especially on a twisty circuit such as

Monaco where long views are not on offer to the driver. Messages in code on boards hung over their pitwall were the long-standing way, listing intervals ahead or behind and the number of laps of the race remaining. But this is old hat now.

The key change was in pit-to-car communication technology with team bosses and tacticians able to radio the driver from the pitwall and vice versa. This doesn't always work, however, with sections of tracks surrounded by trees often blocking the signal.

'Pit now' would have been a sensible call to Jean Alesi when he was racing for Benetton in the 1997 Australian GP, but he failed to hear or heed it and ran out of fuel. Sometimes the problem is both the pit crew and the driver pressing the radio button at the same time and cancelling each other out. At other times, it's the driver's lack of concentration.

Above: ... laps we presume, as indicated to HWM driver Lance Macklin as he motors on towards victory in the International Trophy race at Silverstone

Right: Messages from team to driver are now transmitted via radio from the pitwall. This is BAR's packed 'prat perch' at the 2005 Canadian GP

1966

The chequered flag

IT'S BLACK AND WHITE AND TOTEMIC, a symbol of motor racing the world over. Waved at the race winner and held static for those who are next across the finish line, it's a marker for celebration for the swift and commiseration for those not so fortunate. It's motor racing through and through, unmistakable even for those from other walks of life. It's a potent symbol.

Originally waved down at track level – sometimes seemingly in the middle of the track when the portly Toto Roche used to have the honour of waving it at the French GPs of the early 1960s – the chequered flag has long since been moved upstairs to be displayed from a gantry overhanging the track. This move was made to protect the flag official from the trajectory of the cars racing to the finish line, but it also made the flag more visible to drivers as they flashed past at speeds of up to 170mph, something that was essential to stop them from setting off on an additional lap at unabated speed and perhaps coming across marshals clearing a stranded car, with all the dangers that implies.

Above: Americans have a special knack for being showy, as demonstrated by the flag official as Jim Clark takes victory for Lotus in the 1966 US GP at Watkins Glen

Right: Note how the flag official has long since been moved from trackside and up onto a gantry for his own safety, as shown here at the 2005 French GP

1966

Hitching a lift

HOP ON, BUDDY. Drivers may be enemies when the race is under way, but they can display compassion when the race is over, particularly towards fellow drivers whose cars have broken and who need a ride back to the pits. Shots abound of this happening in the friendly 1960s, when the frequent deaths of contemporaries perhaps made rivals more compassionate, although taking care of hot exhaust pipes made drivers extra vigilant when climbing aboard the rear of a rivals' cars.

Vittorio Brambilla was a driver to avoid, however, as he once offered a lift to a rival and then duly forgot about his charge and returned to the pits at near racing speed, losing his passenger somewhere along the way.

The most famous pick-up of modern times was at the 1991 British GP at Silverstone, when Nigel Mansell offered his pursuer Ayrton Senna a lift home on his Williams' sidepod after the Brazilian dropped out on the final lap when his McLaren ran out of fuel.

Above: He might have been his arch-rival, but Nigel Mansell took pity on Ayrton Senna and let him hop aboard after the Brazilian retired at the end of the 1991 British GP

Left: Holding on to the flimsy windscreen, Lorenzo Bandini cadges a lift back to the pits from Ferrari team-mate Mike Parkes at the 1966 Italian GP at Monza

1953

The art of passing

SLIP UP BEHIND AND POUNCE is the best way to overtake a rival racer, as drivers can never defend against a surprise attack, whereas they can, even if slower, counter an attack that they have seen coming.

In short, overtaking is an art, an essential art if a driver wants to progress to greater things. However, throughout the 1990s, it was something of a lost art as grand prix racing became rather processional, the race order determined more by the quality of the machinery than by the quality of the driver. Indeed, such had been the development of aerodynamics that it had become hard to get close to a car, if chasing, since being in its wake would remove vital downforce from its nose and thus slow the car.

Back in the early 1960s, before cars sprouted aerodynamic wings, cars disturbed less airflow and thus it was easy to get up close and 'hitch a ride' in its slipstream before pulling out on the approach to a corner and easing past, making circuits with long straights, such as Reims and Monza, fabulous for overtaking. Many a classic race was enjoyed at both circuits before the former was dropped on safety grounds and the latter had chicanes inserted. Recently, with wings being limited in size to slow the cars, there has been the added attraction of overtaking again, with Kimi Raikkonen and Fernando Alonso putting on an extraordinary display as they worked their way through the field in the 2005 Japanese Grand Prix.

Left: Getting a tow down the straight is an art. Here, at Monza in 1953, Juan Manuel Fangio attempts to get his Maserati close enough to the Ferraris of Giuseppe Farina and Alberto Ascari to get one

Above: Lewis Hamilton proved a master of passing in his rookie season for McLaren in 2007, taking no prisoners to slash past the leading cars at the Italian GP

1939

Laps of honour

TAKING A BOW is the done thing after a stage play, the opera or the ballet, so why shouldn't it be so after a driver has toiled for nigh on a couple of hours, putting his life on the line, to win a grand prix?

The current modus operandi in this quarter is for the driver to start celebrating as they take the chequered flag, some with a punch of the air, others with a double-handed salute lasting pretty much all of the way around their lap back to the collection area beneath the podium. It's as much for the driver to let off steam as it is to acknowledge the crowd, but it works both ways, with each feeding off the other.

It hasn't always been so, though, as the winner and the two runners-up used to be handed their garlands in a brief ceremony before being driven around the circuit on the back of a car to wave to the crowds.

This was taken a stage further at the British Grand Prix in the 1960s when the winning driver, his car and his team were all loaded onto the back of a flat-bed truck and taken for a triumphal tour. The crowds today would certainly approve of such a parade, sometimes wanting to congratulate the pit crew for a slick stop as much as the driver for winning the grand prix.

Left: Winners were always bedecked with garlands in the 1930s. Rudolf Caracciola salutes in local style after winning the German GP in his Mercedes-Benz W154

Right: The Renault team celebrate en masse as Giancarlo Fisichella climbs out of his Renault R25 after winning the Australian GP in 2005

Picture Credits

All images courtesy of **LAT Photographic**
Special thanks to **Kathy Agar, Zoe Mayho** and **Tim Wright**

Above: Jose Froilan Gonzalez, almost overflowing the cockpit, races to Ferrari's first victory in a World Championship grand prix, at Silverstone in 1951